Wishing you all the very best, Eleanor and Hermann,
from Tom and Gillian with love.

Three Centuries of American Art

Three Centuries of American Art

By Lloyd Goodrich

Published for the
Whitney Museum of American Art
by Frederick A. Praeger, Publishers
New York—Washington—London

Contents

1   From Colonies to Nation   7

2   Expanding Frontiers   24

3   Native and Cosmopolitan   42

4   Modernism and the American Scene   72

5   New Forces   100

    Index   146

Published in the United States of America in 1966
by FREDERICK A. PRAEGER, Inc., Publishers
111 Fourth Avenue, New York, N. Y. 10003
77-79 Charlotte Street, London, W. 1, England
Library of Congress Catalog Card Number: 66-26551

Copyright © 1966 by the Whitney Museum of American Art, New York
Designed by Elton S. Robinson
Printed in the United States of America
by Publishers Printing — Admiral Press, New York

Foreword

This book is not a detailed history of American art, but a pictorial survey, with accompanying text, of painting and sculpture in America from colonial times to the present, as represented by outstanding works, selected on the basis of their artistic qualities and their meaning to us today. They are about equally divided between the twentieth century and earlier centuries — a balance which indicates a belief in the increasing range and vitality of American art in our period. As can be seen, the text concentrates on leading figures of the past and present, while also discussing certain broad tendencies in American art through three centuries. In particular, I have tried to analyze the changing relations between native creativity and international influences.

The book is based on the large historic exhibition, "Art of the United States: 1670-1966," marking the opening of the new building of the Whitney Museum of American Art in 1966. This exhibition was made possible by the generous cooperation of many owners, public and private, who lent important paintings and sculpture from their collections, including a number of works not customarily lent. Because of a simultaneous exhibition staged by the Museum of Early American Folk Arts, this field was represented in the Whitney's show by a limited number of major examples. American sculpture before 1900 was represented by certain key figures, since the majority of its achievements were in monumental sculpture.

I wish to acknowledge the kindness of Jean Lipman, Editor of *Art in America,* for her permission to use in revised form some parts of my article "What Is American in American Art?", originally published in the magazine, and later republished in a book of the same title. L.G.

1 From Colonies to Nation

Art began in the American colonies amid conditions such as existed in none of the European homelands. Instead of civilized societies which had inhabited the same regions for centuries, here were colonists drawn from many countries, settling a vast and little known continent. For the first century and a half, up through the Revolution, the American people were too busy conquering the wilderness and achieving some degree of material civilization, to give much attention to the arts. They had little margin of wealth and leisure, and no long cultural traditions. There were no centralized government, no royal court, no cultivated nobility. The simple churches, both North and South, had no need for religious art; and in New England there was the Puritan condemnation of images. As for historical art, this requires official patronage, which was lacking, and a background of history, which was still short. Classical subjects were even more foreign, and involved the forbidden motif of the nude. The picturing of daily life — what is called genre art — was of no interest to the mercantile aristocracy. (John Greenwood's rowdy *Sea Captains Carousing at Surinam* was an exception that proves the rule.) There was some landscape painting, mostly by folk artists, but a people engaged in a battle with wild nature had little use for the romantic love of nature that is the flower of a more advanced culture.

And in general the educated class was more word-conscious than image-conscious, more verbal-minded than visual-minded. (In this respect, American mores have undergone a basic change in the twentieth century, with the coming of the movies, television, advertising and the picture press.)

Up to the end of the eighteenth century, the only kind of art for which there was any real demand by the upper level of society, was portraiture. The desire to perpetuate one's personal image for one's family and descendants is basic and immemorial, going back to the Pharoahs and earlier. In the English homeland, portrait-painting was by far the most popular form of art. In the words of Benjamin Robert Haydon, the embittered English exponent of the grand style of historical and classical painting: "Portraiture is always independent of art and has little or nothing to do with it. It is one of the staple manufactures of the Empire. Wherever the British settle, wherever they colonize, they carry, and will ever carry, trial by jury, horse-racing, and portrait-painting."

So it was in portraiture that the colonial artists made their first achievements. That in such conditions they produced so many portraits which are not just likenesses but also works of art, is a tribute to man's innate creativity — a proof that no matter how bare the soil, the flower of art is a hardy perennial.

The work of art is a physical object; it exists in only one place. From earliest times Americans possessed the great books of the world, but they had few great works of art until the late nineteenth century. There were engravings, but they were poor substitutes for the originals. No regular art schools existed until the Pennsylvania Academy of the Fine Arts was founded in 1805. For any thorough study one had to go to Europe. In the colonies professional standards were represented by a few artists of European origin and training, who themselves had not been the most successful practitioners in their own countries; as the saying goes, "Dukes do not emigrate."

One exception was John Smibert, who came to America in 1729 and settled in Boston. Though no Hogarth, Smibert had a sound traditional technique, a strong honest sense of character, and a genial humanity. He entirely lacked the elegance of the fashionable British portraitists, making no attempt to flatter or to conceal his sitter's age, homeliness or stoutness. In these respects he belonged to the solid tradition of British provincial portraiture. To the colonies he brought the most professional style that they had seen, and his influence was considerable.

But most of the colonial artists, including some of the best, were self-taught. Many of them were artisans — carpenters, shipwrights, house painters, sign and carriage painters. Some went on to more sophistication, but most remained essentially primitive. Early America had a much larger proportion of folk artists than Europe, even well into the nineteenth century.

The folk artist had certain qualities that the more sophisticated artist had lost. He went straight to the heart of things. Instinctively, without theorizing, he knew that art is not the photographic copying of nature, but the creation of a pictorial equivalent for nature in physical materials — canvas, pigment, stone or wood. He retained the craftsman's respect for the physical substance and structure of the work of art. His eye was an innocent one, concerned more with the object itself than its appearance. He had an innate gift for simplification, for recording the essentials. And he had an instinctive feeling for form and line and color, and the patterns they created. Hence his art, within definite limits, represented something sound and pure.

Most folk art was created directly out of reality, out of local and specific content, which gave it a strong native flavor. Sometimes it contained reminiscences of whatever art its producer might have seen — prints, textiles, porcelain or the instruction books that took the place of art schools. But all this was translated into folk language.

This native flavor appeared early in the untrained limners who painted portraits in the colonies from the middle seventeenth century on. Many of them were travelling artists who went from town to town, sometimes with stock portraits already painted except for the sitter's individual face, hands and accessories. They seldom bothered to sign their works, since they were artisans doing their jobs rather than artists expressing their personalities. So most of them have remained anonymous. But in certain cases, modern scholarship has been able to bring together works obviously by the same hand, and to identify their authorship if not their names.

In style the limners varied from colony to colony and from artist to artist, ranging from the severity of certain New England painters to the naive elegance of the New York and Hudson River artists, such as the anonymous creator of the Van Cortlandt portraits, based on engravings of works by Sir Godfrey Kneller. But they had in common the primitive virtues of honesty, an instinct for color, line and decorative pattern, and above all, the physical integrity that marks the primitive in every age and land.

A pure folk portraitist, and one of the strongest, was Winthrop Chandler of Massachusetts. By trade a house painter, evidently experienced in ornamental painting, Chandler had a sound craft basis for his portraits of his family and friends. Built directly out of the people and surroundings he knew, his pictures showed little or no trace of outside influences. Everything was absolutely solid and tangible, down to the brass tacks (literally) in the upholstery. Faces, bodies and hands had a rocklike strength of character. Powerful outlines defined every shape with complete precision. The queer contorted forms were filled with inner energy. Out of these uncompromising elements Chandler produced overall design of stunning impact and handsomeness.

Even when the artist was more sophisticated, and aped current European styles, the underlying primitive structure remained intact, and the rococo or neo-classic graces superimposed on it were alive and vital. It was this combination of structural strength and naive elegance that gave a unique charm to the work of Feke, Blackburn, Copley and Rush, and to the best in colonial architecture.

Out of the general colonial tradition of face-painting developed the two most gifted native-born painters of the eighteenth century, Robert Feke and John Singleton Copley. Feke's early work was almost as unsophisticated as his predecessors', but with greater skill and refinement. The masterpiece of his early years, *Isaac Royall and His Family,* painted in 1741, was obviously based on Smibert's group portrait of Bishop Berkeley and his entourage, done twelve years earlier, now in the Yale University Art Gallery. But basically the style of Feke's picture was primitive, with none of Smibert's relative cosmopolitanism. In its pure precise forms, its decorative beauty, and the combined severity and refinement characteristic of Feke, it stemmed from the indigenous tradition, of which it is one of the finest examples.

As Feke developed, his skill increased, and he aimed at the elegance of fashionable London portraiture. But he never lost the clarity and sense of form inherited from the native limners. This relative innocence saved him from the current trend of the British school toward the brilliant rendering of visual appearances. His greatest mature work, *Brigadier General Samuel Waldo,* preserved his earlier qualities of form but with an added richness and substance. Shortly after painting it, Feke disappeared from history, probably dying in his middle forties — a loss to early American art.

Our greatest colonial artist, Copley, came out of the same native portrait tradition. Aside from a few years' contact with his artist stepfather, Peter Pelham, Copley was self-taught. His early style was basically that of the provincial limners, raised to a higher level. A fundamental honesty, a fidelity to the truth as he saw it, a firm grasp of the realities of the sitter and his setting, a powerful command of character— these virtues, which he shared with the limners, were combined with a capacity for sculptural form and architectonic design that gave his work, with all its intense realism, a classic order. All this he owed to the native tradition and to his inborn gifts more than to the current British school. Indeed, his style was closer to the combined realism and classicism of his French contemporary Jacques-Louis David, though there is no evidence of influence.

But Copley aspired toward the sophistication of the British school, which he knew through engravings. He resented the restrictions of portrait-painting, and longed to undertake more imaginative subjects. Dissatisfied with provincial Boston, his thoughts turned constantly to the great world of Europe. In 1774, a year before the outbreak of the American Revolution, he left his native land, eventually settling in London. There his earlier realism gave way to a more knowledgeable and skilled style, in which he executed some of the ablest, most attractive portraits of the period; and, of greater importance in the history of art, a series of large historical compositions which were among the most impressive achievements of British painting. But the uncompromising realistic power of his American work declined. With no long native tradition to back him up, too easily impressed by the skill of British portraiture, he exchanged his primitive strength for the graces of the older tradition. Thus America lost her greatest artist, to add another good painter to the British school. It is interesting to speculate on the course of art in the new United States if Copley had returned, as he originally intended. He would have been the unquestioned leader among American artists, and with this prestige he might have enabled them to break through the limitations of portrait-painting and to initiate a broader art.

Copley presents one of the earliest examples of the conflict between the native and the international forces that was to continue in American art through the nineteenth century: between inborn gifts and foreign experience, between the innocent eye and the knowledgeable mind. The tragedy of primitive virtues in the modern world is that they are inevitably doomed to disappear. Their possessor aspires toward more conscious knowledge and skill, and in the process loses more than he gains. This was to happen to many Americans as the surviving primitivism of the colonies gave way to increasing sophistication.

The foremost continuer of the colonial tradition in the new nation was Charles Willson Peale, who after two years in Benjamin West's studio in London returned to his native land, fought in the Revolutionary War, and painted an invaluable series of life portraits of the leaders of the young republic. Endowed with great energy and boundless curiosity, interested in the natural sciences as well as art, Peale in his long busy life became the chief figure of art in Philadelphia, in the 1780's started a picture gallery and the first American museum of natural history, was the prime mover in the establishment of the Pennsylvania Academy of the Fine Arts, and founded a family dynasty of artists, including his sons Raphaelle and Rembrandt. (His *Exhuming the Mastodon* is a record of his excavation of the first skeleton of this prehistoric beast unearthed in America.) As a painter Peale was far in advance of his colonial predecessors (except Copley) in realistic ability, technical competence, mastery of chiaroscuro, and compositional powers. But basically his style was a continuation and maturing of the old native tradition. His sense of character was strong and seldom flattering; his people were often positively homely, and sometimes with an archaic cast of countenance that recalls the limners. The clarity and precision of his style, and its reliance on basic sculptural forms, had interesting parallels with the current French neo-classic school, as in the case of Copley.

A painter who maintained a happy balance between native talent and foreign influence was Ralph Earl of Connecticut. An early portrait such as that of Roger Sherman was obviously the work of a man with little knowledge of other art, but utterly bent on realizing the sitter's physical existence.

In seven years in England Earl acquired more ease, but his sophistication was only skin-deep; within a few years after his return to America he had reverted to his old Yankee self. His sitters might be dressed in their Sunday best, but they had none of the elegance of Romney's or Lawrence's people. To Earl the sitter's personal surroundings were almost as important as the sitter himself. Chief Justice Oliver Ellsworth and his wife are seated in their library, through the window of which, in delightfully incongruous fashion, is a view of the house in which they are. Such actual landscape backgrounds appeared frequently in Earl's paintings. He had more sense of the picture as a whole than most of his professional brethren; to him a portrait was a composition in which figures, furniture, draperies, carpets and landscape all played their parts. Earl's style was basically folk, but enriched by foreign experience, without being submerged by it.

The outstanding case of a colonial who grew to maturity through foreign experience was Gilbert Stuart. Born in Rhode Island, going to London in 1775 at the age of twenty, he absorbed the accumulated skill of the British portrait school in its golden age. After a successful but financially disastrous career in London and Dublin — for he was a great spender — Stuart returned in 1792 to his native land, where he soon became the most popular portraitist of the United States. In England he had acquired a ripeness of artistry beyond any American's of the time: command of the brush, vividness of characterization, mastery of light and shadow, and richness and delicacy of color, especially in his pearly flesh tones. His portraits of women in particular achieved a vivacity and subtlety that made him preeminently an interpreter of the feminine. But there was no Victorian sentimentality in Stuart; he was a product of the robust, high-living eighteenth century.

Stuart's sophistication had a wide and permanent effect on portrait-painting in this country. After him, only folk painters could remain oblivious to the British portrait style. Something of Stuart can be seen in most professional portraitists of the first half of the nineteenth century. Well into the century portraiture retained its predominant position, and produced its masters. In spite of the deadly dullness of the run-of-the-mill product, the school exhibited a wide variety of qualities and skills. To name only a few: the cosmopolitan elegance of Sully, most Victorian of Americans, and one of the most brilliant; the solid character and human warmth of John Neagle, and his rich handling of the brush; the classic order and completeness of Samuel F. B. Morse. In this heyday of portraiture, American artists achieved all degrees of balance between native character, often grim enough, and worldly sophistication. After the mid-century artistic values declined (perhaps under competition with photography), until Thomas Eakins revived portraiture as art.

Sculpture in the colonies and the early republic was much more predominantly folk than painting. For portraits, painting was obviously more lifelike, and more usable in the home. Colonial and federal architecture did not call for sculptural adornment. Public monuments were beyond the ambitions of governments, whether colonial or national. Protestantism had no use for religious sculpture, and the most vital Catholic creations were the painted wooden images produced in the former Spanish colonies in the Southwest, primitive in comparison with the baroque sculpture of the great old cathedrals and churches of Mexico, but filled with a fervid, often macabre vitality.

But even under the least favorable conditions, art will spring up. Wherever a building or a place called for more than the merely utilitarian, sculpture of some kind appeared. Among the earliest were the figurative and decorative carvings on colonial gravestones, touching in their naive awkwardness. This was almost the only stone carving before 1800; the great bulk of folk sculpture was in wood, and what has survived is probably only a fraction of a thriving craft. For a population only partly literate, shop and trade images were essential means of advertising. Weathervanes demanded more than a simple arrow. Until the Civil War a basic American industry was shipbuilding, and the noble functional forms of sailing ships needed figureheads and stern-pieces to complete their beauty. Throughout history seafaring races have produced skilled wood carving, and the figureheads on American ships were among the most inventive sculptures produced in this country. This art form (unfortunately subject to a high degree of loss due to shipwreck and the elements) flourished until the last third of the nineteenth century — until the shift from sail to steam, from wood to iron, and from hand-work to machine-work.

Out of the craft of wood carving, and figureheads in particular, came the foremost early American sculptor, William Rush of Philadelphia — just as Feke and Copley had come out of colonial face-painting. As with them, the basis of Rush's style was primitive, but on this foundation he built a much more highly developed art. The keynote of his work was exuberant vitality, a jocund pagan spirit quite different from the severity of Puritanism. *Comedy* and *Tragedy,* carved in wood (like almost all his pieces) for the exterior of a Philadelphia theater, are an entrancing pair: *Comedy* with her dancing air and come-hither look, *Tragedy* trying to look glum but not succeeding. There was an element of the naive in Rush's style; the flamboyant features and archaic smiles seem provincial caricatures of the Greek ideal. But he was a far more mature artist than the folk carvers, with little of their stiff awkwardness. Conceived in the complete round, his forms were bursting with energy. Bodies, draperies, rippling hair, jaunty upturned breasts, flying ribbons — all were in movement, with a living rhythmic flow of forms. Rush evidently had a sound knowledge of anatomy; his figures were constructed surely, and their voluminous classic robes with elaborate folds were handled in masterly fashion, not muffling the forms beneath but enhancing them. Never inhibited by literal naturalism or cold neo-classicism, his genuine plastic gift expressed itself freely and boldly. American sculpture of the nineteenth century would have presented a livelier picture if it had achieved Rush's combination of native energy with acquired knowledge.

As the young nation began to outgrow colonialism, Europe's magnetic attraction for the American artist increased — perhaps even more than for the American writer. Over there were the masterpieces, the great old cities, and the civilized landscape, mellowed and humanized by centuries of cultivation. By contrast, America was crude, raw, an artistic desert, impossible to assimilate into art. The irresist-

ible trend was toward closer contact with Europe, and with all that Europe represented in art. In the development of American art an essential factor has been the interaction between native creativity, provincial though it might be, and the powerful influence of Europe. Through this interaction some artists have matured, some have been ruined, some have remained impervious.

As the Americans spent more time abroad, the more intelligent of them strove to break away from the routine of portrait-painting and to attempt broader themes: classical, religious or historical. Society back home gave small encouragement to these aspirations; and it was abroad, in the London studio of Benjamin West, that the first American attempts at the grand style originated. West, American by birth but settling permanently in London in 1763, becoming president of the Royal Academy and court painter to George III, nevertheless remained American in his sympathies. In subject-matter he was an innovator, picturing contemporary history earlier than David or Baron Gros, and romantic themes earlier than Prud'hon, Géricault or Delacroix. His huge compositions were conscientious rather than inspired adaptations of the old masters, theatrical in sentiment, conventional in composition, and deadly dull in execution. They recall Byron's cruel gibe:

> . . . *the dotard West,*
> *Europe's worst dauber, and poor England's best.*

Nevertheless, West was to prove a forerunner of romanticism. His lead in contemporary history was carried on by Copley in his large compositions painted in England, with a vitality surpassing West. It is interesting that these two pioneers of historical painting were both American-born.

West was a busy teacher, especially kind to young Americans, and through his hospitable London studio passed many of the Americans who attempted historical and classical subjects. Charles Willson Peale had studied with him in the 1760's. It was under West's teaching that John Trumbull painted his first Revolutionary battle scenes in the 1780's. Though small in scale, they show a dramatic sense and an ability to handle compositions of many figures in movement and in varying lights, that still rank them as the finest American historical paintings in the grand style. On his return to the United States, Trumbull undertook a career of picturing American history. To this end he painted many portrait studies of famous public figures, and tried to persuade the federal government to commission large versions of his scenes of the Revolution. But our government had advanced little beyond the colonial administrations in recognition of the arts, and by the time Trumbull finally secured commissions for four large wall paintings in the rotunda of the Capitol in Washington, his youthful fire was gone; the results have little of the life of the small London versions.

The case of Washington Allston most clearly reveals the problem of the imaginative artist in early nineteenth-century America. The most cultivated mind in our art of the time, Allston spent the impressionable years of young manhood in Italy, in contact with antiquity and the Renaissance, and with the Italian landscape; then seven years in London, where he painted some of his finest works, including *The Rising of a Thunderstorm at Sea* and *Elijah in the Desert.* These early paintings reveal a born romantic poet, a lover of the wild, the lonely and the terrible. But Allston's romanticism was controlled by a sense of tradition, and an ambition to emulate the old masters in the greatest themes. His classical, allegorical and religious compositions were among the most impressive attempts in the Anglo-American world to revive the Renaissance. They would have won him the presidency of the Royal Academy if he had not decided to return to his native country. But actually, Allston's temperament was unsuited for such ambitious undertakings. The essence of his artistic gift was the true romantic poetry of nature, wild and pure, that appeared in his early landscapes. But in his formal compositions this emotion evaporated. After his return to America in middle age, his art showed a progressive loss of energy. He was an artist who needed contact with the great art of the past, but over here he found none — no great paintings, no connoisseurs, no colleagues with anything like his knowledge. And he was incapable of drawing artistic nourishment from the raw material of American life, as his more provincial successors were able to do.

For years he labored in vain to finish his ambitious compositions; while his nostalgic Italian scenes were clearly a reaction from the artistic barrenness of his native land. His career was the reverse of Copley's: with the latter, native vitality was lost in acquiring European sophistication, whereas with Allston, romantic emotion and great intentions were starved by separation from Europe — the response of two opposite temperament to the magnetism of Europe.

The same fate overtook others who essayed imaginative themes. There was John Vanderlyn, studying in Paris under a pupil of David, coming home with the hope of founding a school of American historical art like the Napoleonic one, and ending as an embittered provincial face-painter. And there was Samuel F. B. Morse, friend and pupil of Allston in London, and a highly endowed individual. Morse returned to this country full of ambition, as he said, "to be among those who will revive the splendor of the fifteenth century." But he soon discovered that the classical pictures he had painted abroad were admired, but that nobody bought them. By necessity he became a portrait-painter, and one of the most distinguished, for Morse had a vitality that Allston and Vanderlyn lacked — a realistic grasp of character, a sensuous enjoyment of the visible world — combined with a gift for design that gave his portraits, such as *The Muse,* a fine largeness and balance. But in middle life Morse abandoned the ungrateful career of a moderately paid portraitist to devote the rest of his life to his invention of the telegraph.

So ended the first idealistic attempts to found an American school of classical, religious and allegorical art based on the great European tradition. Not that such noble efforts ceased altogether; but they were mostly carried on by artists who had a solid material base in portrait-painting, such as Charles Willson Peale, Thomas Sully and Rembrandt Peale; and they centered less on classical subjects than on recent American history, and especially on the father image of George Washington. When artistic subject-matter broadened in the second quarter of the nineteenth century, it was not in the direction of the grand style but in more familiar native fields.

ANONYMOUS: *Mrs. Elizabeth Paddy Wensley.*
1670-1680. Oil. 42¼ x 33¾.
Pilgrim Society.

ANONYMOUS: *Portrait of John Van Cortlandt.*
c. 1731. Oil. 57 x 40^{15}/$_{16}$.
The Brooklyn Museum.

ROBERT FEKE: *Isaac Royall and His Family.*
1741. Oil. 56¾₁₆ x 77¾.
Harvard University Law School.

JOHN DURAND: *The Rapalje Children.*
c. 1768. Oil. 50¾ x 40.
The New-York Historical Society.

JOHN SINGLETON COPLEY: *Mr. and Mrs. Thomas Mifflin.*
1773. Oil. 60½ x 48.
Historical Society of Pennsylvania.

JOHN SINGLETON COPLEY: *Mrs. Ezekiel Goldthwait.*
1771. Oil. 50 x 40.
Museum of Fine Arts, Boston.

WILLIAM RUSH: *Comedy.*
1808. Pine. 114 high.
The Edwin Forrest Home.

WILLIAM RUSH: *Tragedy.*
1808. Pine. 114 high.
The Edwin Forrest Home.

JOHN TRUMBULL: *Sortie of the British Garrison at Gibraltar.* c. 1788. Oil. 20 x 30. Cincinnati Art Museum.

CHARLES WILLSON PEALE: *Exhuming the Mastodon.* 1806. Oil. 50 x 62½. The Peale Museum.

WASHINGTON ALLSTON: *Elijah in the Desert.*
1818. Oil. 48¾ x 72½.
Museum of Fine Arts, Boston.

RALPH EARL: *Chief Justice Oliver Ellsworth
and his Wife, Abigail Wolcott.*
1792. Oil. 75¹⁵⁄₁₆ x 86¾.
Wadsworth Atheneum.

GILBERT STUART: *Mrs. Perez Morton.*
c. 1802. Oil. 29 1/16 x 24 1/8.
Worcester Art Museum.

2 Expanding Frontiers

With the rise of Jacksonian democracy in the late 1820's came a new nationalist consciousness. Colonial deference to Europe gave way to an equally provincial belief in the United States as the greatest nation on earth. Westward expansion was bringing a realization of the vast scale and natural wonders of the continent. In the East, the old colonial aristocracy was being replaced by an urban bourgeoisie whose interest in art, though limited, went beyond the perpetuation of their own and their families' faces. Artists and their patrons began to turn toward broader subjects — toward nature as revealed by the expanding frontiers, and toward the contemporary life of the United States.

Some landscape painting had been done in America since early days, but mostly by folk artists, or as the occasional recreation of portraitists. Ralph Earl, one of the first professionals to show a genuine love of nature, not only included landscape backgrounds in his portraits but took time off to paint several pure landscapes. Trumbull, Vanderlyn and Morse painted a few landscapes, including views of Niagara Falls, which was to become a perennial subject. In the late eighteenth century several English painters of decorative landscapes arrived, including William Groombridge, George Beck, William Winstanley and Francis Guy. The most original was Guy, who specialized in Maryland country estates, with little figures of the owner and his family promenading, painted with delicate precision. For him, and for Thomas Birch of Philadelphia, landscape was still topographical, the portraiture of places instead of people. But by the 1810's pure landscape had a few more precursors such as Thomas Doughty and Alvin Fisher.

The first definite school of professional landscape painting did not appear until the middle 1820's — what came to be called the Hudson River school. The man who can be considered its founder was not native-born. Thomas Cole, English by birth, coming to America at seventeen, spent his youth in what were then the virgin forests of Ohio. Highly romantic, strongly religious, and with a decided literary bent, Cole on coming to New York in 1825 found a cultural climate favorable to the growth of landscape, what with Washington Irving's tales of the Hudson River valley, James Fenimore Cooper's novels of the wilderness, and William Cullen Bryant's solemn nature poetry.

To his celebration of the American wilderness, still unravaged, Cole brought a romantic imagination, a love of solitude, and a realization of the spaciousness and grandeur of this new world. He was the first to picture the wilderness with the passion of a poet, and to capture the wild beauty of the continent as it was a century and a half ago. As his friend Bryant wrote after Cole's early death: "I well remember what an enthusiasm was awakened by these early works of his — the delight which was expressed at the opportunity of contemplating pictures which carried the eye over scenes of wild grandeur peculiar to our country, over our aerial mountain-tops, with their mighty growth of forests never touched by the axe, along the banks of streams never deformed by culture, and into the depths of skies bright with the hues of our own climate; skies such as few but Cole could ever paint, and through the transparent abysses of which it seemed that you might send an arrow out of sight."

From the first Cole introduced a more living concept of landscape: a feeling for the life in nature, for her alterations of storm and peace, of clouds and serene light — the whole spectacle of the wilderness and its changing aspects, presented with a new dramatic sense and technical skill. Sometimes his Byronic fantasy led him from the sublime to the ridiculous. Often a religious element appeared, for Cole was concerned not only with nature for herself but as a setting for moralistic allegories. His series of paintings such as *The Departure* and *The Return* (a knight gaily leaving his castle in the morning and borne home lifeless in the evening), or *The Course of Empire*, tracing in five acts the rise, splendor and ruin of an imaginary ancient capital, illustrated his thoughts on the vanity of worldly power and pleasure, and the inevitable destruction that overtakes them. Most of these works were pure Hollywood, but in his finest series, *The Voyage of Life*, he achieved powerful pictorial drama. An artist capable of deplorable corniness, he also created the most vital landscape painting so far in America.

Next to Cole as a leader of the Hudson River school was Asher B. Durand. With him, Cole's flamboyant imagination was replaced by a sober affection for nature. His painstaking hand recorded every detail — the lichened tree trunks, the vine-covered rocks, the flowers and weeds in the foreground. His engaging *Kindred Spirits,* showing Cole and Bryant in a mountain landscape, painted the year after Cole's death, was a memorial, like the poet's tribute to their mutual friend.

Cole's grandiose romanticism and Durand's literal naturalism were the chief influences on the younger painters of the Hudson River school. These artists formed a consciously native school — the first in American art. Many of them were friends, going on walking and sketching trips together in the Catskills, the Adirondacks and the White

Mountains. They were tremendously proud of America's natural beauties — the grandeur of her mountains, the wildness of her forests, the blazing colors of her autumn foliage. Though most of them visited Europe to paint its picturesque places, sometimes remaining for years, their admiration for their own land remained undimmed.

The Hudson River valley proved only the beginning of their exploration of the continent. Some of them, particularly Frederic E. Church, Albert Bierstadt and Thomas Moran, pushed westward to paint the Rocky Mountains, the Grand Canyon and the falls of the Yosemite. Indeed, Church explored much of the western hemisphere: the volcanoes of Mexico, the tropical jungles of South America, the snow-covered peaks of the Andes, the icebergs of Labrador.

The artistic philosophy of these painters was uncomplicated. They believed that painting was primarily the representation of the external world; that the nobler the subject was, the nobler the picture would be; and that the way to express their genuine love of nature was to paint her with absolute fidelity to facts, and in full detail. In the typical Hudson River landscape the canvas is enormous, the viewpoint panoramic; yet so meticulous is the handling that one can count every leaf. In the huge paintings of Church, Bierstadt and Moran, with which the school's grandiose tendencies culminated, the technical proficiency is astounding. Their panoramas were even more extensive than Cole's, while every detail, the exact character of every growing thing, every phenomenon of light and atmosphere and weather, were rendered with more than photographic accuracy.

The artistic limitations of the school were obvious enough. Though contemporaries of the French romantics and the Barbizon school, they showed no awareness of the new trends that were transforming European art, or else they were definitely opposed; to them even Corot was still a revolutionary. Compared to trends in France, their artistic concepts were anachronistic. Their romanticism took the form of literal representation of romantic subjects, rather than expression of romantic emotion in the language of form and color, as with Géricault and Delacroix.

But their direct contact with nature, their observation, and their skill of eye and hand, are values that have endured. In the wide-ranging works of Bierstadt, for example, especially in his less pretentious or highly finished canvases, one continually meets with fresh, unconventional recording of light, color and weather — the work of an acute visual observer. And Church, in a painting like *Twilight in the Wilderness,* achieved color as daring as any optical painter today. If these men had been less committed to literal naturalism, if they had trusted their visual sensations more, their contribution would have been a less baffling combination of art and non-art.

In their best landscapes the character of the American land, its spaciousness and solitude, the clearness of its air, the brilliance of its light, its high remote skies, were pictured truly and with a romantic emotion that is still alive. Their works had a leisurely completeness, a feeling for nature in her myriad aspects, tragic as well as smiling, and a sense of her solid substance and moving forces, rather than her mere appearances — qualities that were lost in the more intimate, fragmentary landscapes of their successors. Ridiculed by later generations, these painters have been rediscovered in our day. They deserve honor not only as pioneer visual explorers of the continent, but as our first nature poets.

Certain other landscapists, not members of the Hudson River school but with the same general viewpoint, produced works of highly personal vision. Fitz Hugh Lane's modest views of quiet harbors and inlets along the Massachusetts and Maine coast, painted with exquisite preciseness, were pervaded by a calm serenity. Somewhat similar were Martin J. Heade's coastal scenes, in which the sense of loneliness, of all-embracing light, of crystalline clarity, attained a penetrating intensity. But Heade's temperament had other sides: the rich romantic profusion of his tropical landscapes such as *View of Tree Fern Walk, Jamaica:* the exotic beauty of his series of South American orchids and hummingbirds; the brooding sensuousness of his flower still-lifes; the threatening drama of *Storm over Narragansett.* His sensibility, different from the objectivity of the Hudson River painters, foretold the future development of American landscape.

That huge historic phenomenon, the westward expansion, brought forth an art all its own, partly reportorial, partly artistic. The early nineteenth-century exploring expeditions were usually accompanied by artists serving also as topographical draftsmen. As the continent was opened up, more and more such visual recorders visited the West. The tremendous scale of the country, the wide horizons and serene monotony of the Great Plains, the hordes of wild animals still roaming the wilderness, the mysterious alien life of the Indians — all this was virgin subject-matter, without precedent in Europe or the East, and seeming to call for a new artistic vision. The pioneer explorer-artist George Catlin was inspired by this world so much vaster and wilder than the East to paint it in a style whose unconventional directness and candor captured some of its majesty. His successors such as Seth Eastman, Alfred J. Miller, Charles Deas and Charles Wimar drew and painted first-hand records that are invaluable historically, though translated into more conventional romantic terms.

Another kind of explorer was John James Audubon. French in ancestry and upbringing, he came to the United States in his youth and spent years roaming the wilderness, gathering material for his two monumental books on the birds and quadrupeds of North America. His watercolor originals were among the first great achievements in this medium, which had been practised mostly by amateurs and designers of colored prints. Audubon was both scientist and artist, but there was no conflict, for the scientist was an observer rather than a theorist, and the artist, while concerned with recording natural facts, was keenly alive to the beauty of nature, and especially to that of birds, the most decorative of living creatures. He was one of the first to picture them as alive and in motion, and in their natural habitats. In his watercolors the forms were large and sculptural, the line bold, the color of utmost purity and strength. Everything was drawn with complete precision, down to the most exquisite details. Audubon had a superb decorative gift; the birds' plumage and markings, and the profusion of foliage, flowers and fruit in which he framed them, created magnificent designs. His sense of form and ordered design linked him with the neo-classicism of David, with whom he had studied for a brief period in Paris.

The development of landscape was paralleled by that of genre painting. Both were products of Jacksonian democracy's new nationalist consciousness. To the old colonial and federal aristocracy the life of the masses had not appeared an appropriate subject for art. But the new democracy brought a sense of the importance of the common man. To artists and the rising bourgeoisie, the everyday life of the American people no longer seemed too vulgar a subject for art.

As with landscape, there had been some occasional genre painting before the 1830's. Francis Guy had produced a few lively city scenes with crowds of townspeople, curiously like Bruegel's. About 1810 John Lewis Krimmel began picturing the life of Philadelphia in small precise watercolors and oils. It is recorded that he received few commissions, as "works of the species he delighted in were not sought after by the wealthy patrons of art." Sometimes

portraitists would break away from their regular occupation to do genre pictures, such as the two lovely conversation pieces, *The Tea Party* and *The Dinner Party*, by Henry Sargent of Boston, painted about 1820.

The first native-born painter to devote himself chiefly to genre was William Sidney Mount, who about 1830 began to paint the people and events of his Long Island farm community. Few artists have created their art so completely out of the life around them. Mount was what is known as a "character"— full of Yankee notions, an amateur musician, an inventor of sorts, and in later years a spiritualist. (He once produced a long letter which he claimed to have received from Rembrandt.) Several times patrons offered to send him abroad, but he always declined. Yet he was surprisingly aware of older European art, especially the Dutch Little Masters.

Mount's paintings of his friends and neighbors were marked by kindly humor, good temper, and an unsentimental love of country life. He had a singularly fresh eye, and his outdoor scenes show keen observation of weather and season and light, and the subtleties of open-air color. A skillful draftsman and handler of the brush, he was one of the most accomplished American painters of his time. His art was an authentic expression of the agrarian democracy of mid-nineteenth-century America, before the impact of industrialism.

An equally promising talent, cut short by early death, was that of Richard Caton Woodville, son of an old Maryland family, who had an opportunity to see Dutch genre pictures in Baltimore, went on to study in Düsseldorf, and on his return devoted himself to painting native city and rural scenes. His little canvases, all too few, were rich in character, with a precise skill rivalling that of the seventeenth-century Dutch masters of genre.

Out in Missouri in the same years, George Caleb Bingham was painting the vigorous, lusty life of the Mississippi River and its people — that life later described so eloquently by Mark Twain. A local product like Mount, Bingham was almost entirely self-taught, but with natural gifts that triumphed over this lack. Like Mount's his art grew directly out of the actualities of the life he knew — the tough, rollicking Mississippi boatmen, the trappers of the Missouri River region, the excitements and racy humors of local politics. His work was realistic, based on first-hand observation; but it also had poetry — the poetry of the great river, its wide expanses and unfolding vistas, seen in varying hours and lights, with a pervading sense of calm, golden serenity.

Bingham was a strong draftsman; everything in his pictures was solidly constructed in three dimensions. Out of the raw material of pioneer life he built complex designs that had a classic order and balance.

By the 1840's the native genre school was flourishing. As was natural in a nation still largely agricultural, country life furnished the favorite themes: rural dances, corn-husking and apple-paring parties, goose raffles, turkey shoots, the hardships and comforts of wintertime. The old-fashioned farm was still the background of a large part of the population, even those who had moved to the cities. Most of the artists had been country boys, as had many of their patrons; and their pictures offered an escape from the growing complexity and ugliness of city life into what was remembered as a simpler and purer world. This nostalgia for the farm was an important element of the nineteenth-century American mind, in both art and literature.

A similar nostalgia was revealed in the many childhood scenes, again a recurring motif in writing and art, and one that produced its masterpieces, such as *Tom Sawyer, Little Women* and *Huckleberry Finn*. Like the writers, the artists of the mid-century were drawn to childhood and country life more than to the disturbing new America of cities and factories and railroads.

The city found little place in their work. In these days when our cities were growing so tremendously, there was no American Daumier to record their teeming life. Our towns of the time were no beauty spots; aside from their older residential sections and a few public buildings and parks that gave some evidence of planning, they were chaotic, squalid and monotonous. There was little in the United States that could be compared with the harmonious beauty of Rome or Paris. To reveal our cities in all their disorderly vitality would have required a more drastic realism than our artists possessed. It remained for the illustrators and the makers of popular prints to create the most complete pictorial record of the urban United States.

Of the vast industrialization that was beginning to transform America there was little trace in our painting. Even the epic of railroad building was recorded by printmakers and illustrators rather than painters. Art needs time to assimilate such tremendous social and technological changes. Even in Europe, the Industrial Revolution produced little industrial subject-matter. Few artists heeded Courbet's admonition in 1861 to paint "railway stations, engine houses, mines and factories. These are the saints and miracles of the nineteenth century." The machine as a subject for art was

not to come into its own until the twentieth century, with cubism, futurism and constructivism.

So most mid-nineteenth-century genre painters focussed on country life, childhood, and the home. Even in their rural scenes, everyday work was not often shown. Bingham's boatmen were rollicking, Mount's farmers were fiddling or dancing or taking their "nooning", Eastman Johnson's country people were engaged in community activities when work took on a festival character. There was none of Millet's intensely serious picturing of the hard daily labor that was the central fact of the farmer's existence. Nor was their any sign of the elements of decay in agricultural life: the exodus of young people to the cities, the abandoned farm. These artists were painting American farm life as it was in its golden days, and their art expressed an optimism that we like to think of as characteristically American.

Naturally, there was no satire on the established order. As one critic said, Eastman Johnson's pictures of rural workers "preached no ugly doctrine of discontent." Sex played little part except in the sublimated form of Victorian sentiment. A devotion to the family and domestic virtues was always in evidence. Occasionally there were glimpses of the alcoholic capacity of the American male, but the public lip-service to temperance was generally respected. There was much humor, of a genial, good-natured kind, without edge or earthiness. Compared to current European painting of contemporary life — Courbet, Millet, Daumier — ours was singularly innocent. It was the art of a young, growing democracy, optimistic and expansive, idealistic in even its most naturalistic phases.

One of the few exceptions to the general idyllicism was David G. Blythe, eccentric self-taught satirist of the raw growing town of Pittsburgh. As a person Blythe was a local character — a rolling stone, addicted to alcohol, and to writing satirical or sentimental doggerel. He had a sardonic humor rare at the time — a relish for the ridiculous, for odd characters, for the low comedy of drinking and vagabondage. It was an art straight out of the life of the people, passing no moral judgments, delighting in the squalor and knavery of a crude society, pleased equally with the spectacle of a lawyer hypnotizing a jury and a boy picking pockets. Blythe was an uneven artist, but his best work had a spark of genius. Something of the spirit of Bruegel, Adrian Brouwer and Hogarth reappeared in this nineteenth-century American — in his grotesque originality of form with its curiously knowing distortions, in the wit that presented only the essentials, and above all in that strain of caricatural madness that marks the genuine satirist in every age and country.

A generation earlier had appeared another highly individual painter of American life, of the past rather than the present — John Quidor of New York. His themes were almost entirely literary, mostly from Washington Irving's *Tales of a Traveller* and *Diedrich Knickerbocker's History of New York*, and the novels of Cooper. Irving's mock-heroic account of the Dutch in New York and the eeriness of his *Legend of Sleepy Hollow* found perfect pictorial expression in Quidor's rich humor and imaginative fantasy. His style matched his content: baroque, elaborate in details and conceits, filled with energy and movement. Everything was in motion, from Ichabod Crane's gawky dancing figure with flying coat-tails to the twisting arabesques of trees and foliage, as instinct with life as the people. The movement in Quidor's compositions was not merely the representation of moving figures, but movement of the forms themselves. His baroque design was related to seventeenth-century Flemish and Dutch painting, as was his technique of translucent glazes with forms defined by sure, delicate drawing with the brush, and his golden brown color, completely coordinated with the forms. That such a creative traditionalist should appear in the United States of the time is one of the mysteries of American art.

The native genre tradition was continued, with mature artistry, by Eastman Johnson. After thorough study in Germany and Holland, Johnson returned to apply his seasoned technical knowledge to native subject-matter. His range was wide: domestic city life, in which he anticipated Thomas Eakins; country occupations and recreations; the world of childhood. A series of scenes in the spring maple-sugar camps of his native Maine, when whole communities joined in the work and festivities, were marked by unhackneyed observation, and a relish for local idiosyncrasies and the atmosphere of merrymaking — something not usually associated with staid New England. Their freedom of handling and awareness of light showed Johnson breaking away from the tightness of his predecessors toward a more painterly style.

With the increasing cosmopolitanism of the later nineteenth century, and the new aesthetic that condemned the story-telling picture, the old genre school became passé. Its tradition was carried on by anecdotalists such as Thomas Waterman Wood with his country-store cracker-barrel subjects, J. G. Brown with his angelic scrubbed newsboys, and E. L. Henry with his charming idylls of oldtime New York or of a rustic society that was already disappearing. In its

sentimental fixation on the past their work was purely a survival, and a decline from the robust contemporary genre of the mid-century. Not until the twentieth century, with the appearance of the New York realists, the regionalists, and the painters of the American scene, was the life of the people to become once more a vital theme for artists.

Still-life painting had appeared early in America, in ornamental flower and fruit pieces by folk artists and amateurs. The prodigious Peale family had produced a succession of accomplished still-life painters: Charles Willson's sons Raphaelle and Rubens, his brother James, and the latter's three daughters. Their paintings and those of other painters of the time were related in a general way to seventeenth-century Dutch still-life: objects decorative, appetizing or sensuously pleasing, grouped on tables, giving the artist an opportunity to realize to the full their forms, colors and textures, without the distracting personality of a sitter. The Peales were addicted to *trompe l'oeil* painting; Charles Willson's remarkable *Staircase Group*, featuring Raphaelle and Titian Ramsay Peale on a stairway, was exhibited inside an actual door frame with a wooden step projecting below — which, it is said, caused George Washington to bow courteously to the two figures as he passed. Raphaelle's *After the Bath*, a suspended white sheet behind which, above and below, appeared a girl's bare arm and foot, was realistic enough to enrage the artist's wife when she first saw it in his studio. Beyond this, it was a work of art in its clear, precise painting of the folds of drapery. Of all the Peales, Raphaelle's modest small still-lifes, with their sensuous bloom and penetrating mood, were the most personal and finely realized.

Story-telling still-life, assembling objects that had meanings beyond their physical qualities, was practised early by Charles Bird King: in his case, things with associations personal to the artist, such as unpaid bills and the notice of a sheriff's sale. This vein of visual jokes and metaphors was exploited fully by the flourishing and popular *trompe l'oeil* school of the 1880's and 1890's, with their letter-racks and facsimiles of paper currency.

The Philadelphia still-life tradition was carried to its fullest development by William M. Harnett. His objects were generally fine in quality, luxurious, often exotic; the belongings of a cultivated gentleman. His vision was crystal-clear; every detail was rendered with microscopic fidelity. Forms were deceptively three-dimensional, completely round and situated in deep space. To these standard characteristics of *trompe l'oeil* Harnett added a sense of formal relations, a mastery of complex design, and a severe distinction of style that raised his art above the average of the school.

Harnett's chief disciple and rival was John F. Peto, who differed in his preoccupation with things of humble everyday use, and especially with worn, cast-off and dilapidated objects such as one sees in junk-shop windows. His pictures revealed a strain of burlesque humor foreign to Harnett. Light played a major role, producing dramatic contrasts of lights and shadows. Peto's still-lifes convey a sense of stillness, abandonment, expectancy — a poignant intensity of mood.

The fantastic possibilities of *trompe-l'oeil,* its ingenious assembling of objects with far-reaching associations and implications, were pushed to the furthest extreme by John Haberle, whose inventiveness and startling technical feats anticipated surrealism.

Until the early nineteenth century such sculpture as existed in the United States was still mostly folk. But from the 1820's on more professionals emerged. Facilities for learning their art were even more meager than for painting, and inevitably most of them went abroad to study, almost invariably to Italy, where they found not only the great works of the past but skilled Italian craftsmen who could teach them to carve stone, and could assist them in turning plaster models into marble. Settling in Rome or Florence, they remained for years, and in many cases for the rest of their lives.

In Italy there was not only the overwhelming past but the current neo-classic school of Canova and his successor Thorwaldsen. Little equipped to withstand such pressures, the Americans without exception adopted the neo-classic formulas. Mythological or allegorical themes were embodied in innumerable white marble female nudes based on Greek and Roman originals. But in the hands of the Americans, the Venus de' Medici was converted to virginal chastity. In American painting the nude was still questionable, but when Hiram Powers' immaculate *Greek Slave* was exhibited in the United States in 1847, with her purity vouched for by a committee of the clergy, she attracted crowds. Taste had changed in the republic, and neo-classicism triumphed in sculpture as it had not in painting.

By the 1840's there was a vogue for sculpture. The rich American visiting Italy was proud to have a fellow American carve his marble bust, barechested, or if he was eminent enough, togaed; and perhaps also to bring home an "ideal" figure for the parlor. Sculpture had become a lucrative profession. Replicas by Italian stonecarvers were turned out by the scores, and in some cases by the hundreds.

There were exceptions to the general vacuousness, such as Horatio Greenough, whose prophetic essays on art were a more adequate expression of his brilliant mind than most of his sculpture. His colossal figure of Washington commissioned for the Capitol, showing the father of his country half-nude, in the pose of the Olympian Zeus, was nevertheless one of the few impressive early American monuments. And that study in Italy was not an absolute necessity was proved by Erastus D. Palmer of Albany, N. Y., who did not go abroad until he was almost sixty, yet created in *The White Captive* a completely neo-classic work, and one of the finest, for Palmer had breathed life into a conventional concept.

But by far the most original sculptor of the period was William Rimmer of Boston, who was also a self-taught physician, a learned anatomist, a magnetic teacher, an imaginative romantic painter, and a great draftsman. Rimmer was a traditionalist; his subjects were Greek, Roman, Shakespearean or purely imaginary, his style was a blend of classic and Renaissance. But his was a living traditionalism. With him neo-classic frigidity was replaced by depth and intensity of emotion, love of the heroic, and a deep-seated sense of the tragic. His whole art, whether in sculpture, painting or drawing, was based on the human or animal body. Anatomical mastery was evident in everything he created, but it was not merely intellectual mastery. There was sheer physical power in his figures; they were instinct with energy, with muscular tensions, with movement. Rimmer had that rare gift, genuine plastic creativity, which gives his few surviving works a lasting vitality. Relatively obscure as an artist during his lifetime (his three finest pieces were not cast in bronze until twenty-five years after his death) he seems closer to us today than any of his contemporaries.

By the 1860's American sculpture had acquired professional status, but its achievements so far, with a few exceptions, had been in gaining technical skill and contact with Europe and the art of the past, rather than in original creation.

THOMAS COLE: *The Oxbow (The Connecticut River near Northampton).*
1836. Oil. 51½ x 76.
The Metropolitan Museum of Art.

SAMUEL F. B. MORSE: *The Muse — Susan Walker Morse.*
c. 1835-1837. Oil. 73¾ x 57⅝.
The Metropolitan Museum of Art.

ASHER B. DURAND: *Kindred Spirits*.
1849. Oil. 44 x 36.
The New York Public Library.

ALBERT BIERSTADT: *The Buffalo Trail —*
The Impending Storm.
1869. Oil. 29½ x 49½.
The Corcoran Gallery of Art.

ARTIN J. HEADE: *View of Tree Fern Walk, Jamaica.*
887. Oil. 53 x 90.
ollection of Patrick A. Doheny.

DAVID G. BLYTHE: *The Pittsburgh Horse Market.*
c. 1858. Oil. 26½ x 36½.
Collection of Thomas M. Evans.

GEORGE CALEB BINGHAM: *Raftsmen Playing Cards.*
1847. Oil. 28 x 36.
City Art Museum of St. Louis.

WILLIAM SIDNEY MOUNT: *Eel Spearing at Setauket.*
1845. Oil. 29 x 36.
New York State Historical Association.

FREDERIC EDWIN CHURCH: *Rainy Season in the Tropics.*
1866. Oil. 55 x 84.
Collection of Mr. and Mrs. J. William Middendorf II.

EDWARD HICKS: *The Peaceable Kingdom.*
1840-1845. Oil. 30⅛ x 34½.
New York State Historical Association.

EDWIN ROMANZO ELMER:
Mourning Picture.
1889. Oil. 28 x 36.
Smith College Museum of Art.

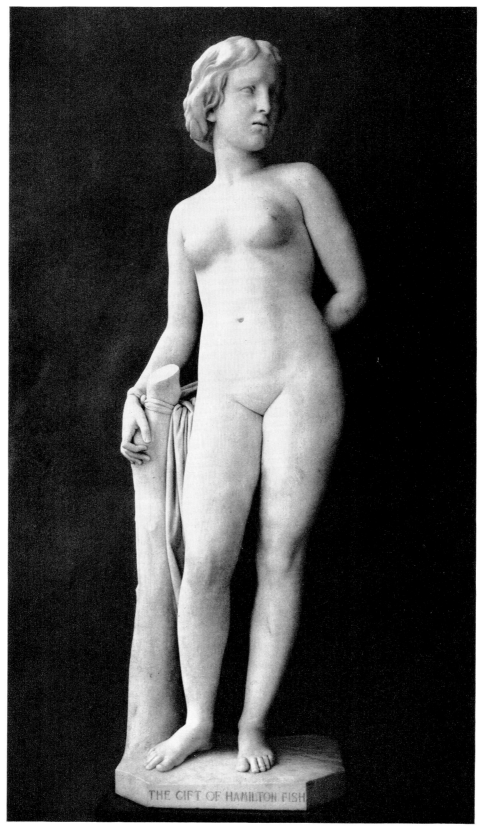

ERASTUS DOW PALMER: *The White Captive.*
1859. Marble. 66 high.
The Metropolitan Museum of Art.

WILLIAM RIMMER: *The Dying Centaur.*
c. 1871. Bronze. 21½ high.
The Metropolitan Museum of Art.

WILLIAM M. HARNETT: *After the Hunt.*
1885. Oil. 71 x 48.
California Palace of the Legion of Honor.

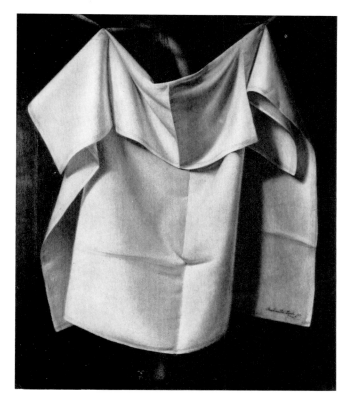

RAPHAELLE PEALE: *After the Bath.*
1823. Oil. 29 x 24.
Nelson Gallery — Atkins Museum.

JOHN HABERLE: *A Bachelor's Drawer.*
1890-1894. Oil. 20 x 36.
Collection of Mr. and Mrs. J. William Middendorf II.

3 Native and Cosmopolitan

For the United States the last third of the nineteenth century was a period of tremendous expansion — in industry, private wealth, cosmopolitanism and cultural sophistication. In art it was a period of new forces and influences. Traditional concepts of the nature and meaning of art were transformed. From the old idea of painting as literal representation or story-telling, the emphasis shifted to subjective expression, to visual sensation, to new ways of feeling and seeing.

The American art world of one hundred years ago was still dominated by the Hudson River school generation. But already a new kind of landscape was taking shape in the work of George Inness and his younger contemporaries Homer Martin and Alexander Wyant. All three began in the Hudson River tradition, but as they matured they developed a fundamentally different vision. With them, landscape became subjective, concerned more with personal emotions than external facts. Their attitude toward nature was Wordsworthian rather than Byronic; to them she was a presence, a being who embodied man's deepest emotions, and whose changing moods were inseparable from his own. The cult of the wilderness was replaced by a feeling for cultivated landscape, the panoramic viewpoint by an intimate one, meticulous detail by breadth and simplification, photographic literalism by a more painterly style. There was a new awareness of the subtleties of changing light and atmosphere. Color and tonal values became more important. This growth in artistic sensibility was assisted by the example of the Barbizon school, expecially Corot.

Inness had begun in the 1840's with a style close to the Hudson River school. But as he developed he concentrated on expressing subjective emotion and on capturing nature's evanescent moods, in a style more and more tonal and chromatic. This growth was assisted by two early visits to Italy and another to France, when he saw the work of the Barbizon painters. Inness' emotionalism occasionally verged on sentimentality; he might be called the Longfellow of landscape, expressing sentiments which were sometimes stirring, sometimes banal. Nevertheless he was the most vital and varied landscapist of his period, and the one who did most to revolutionize native landscape.

Under the influence of Inness and the Barbizon school, Wyant evolved from his tight early style to a reserved silvery tonalism. Homer Martin, who grew up among the Adirondack and Catskill mountains, began painting this wild country in the old literal style. But from the first he revealed a different sensibility, an intimate poetry which was confirmed by the Barbizon example during a stay in France. The keynote of his art, like that of so much early American landscape, was solitude. Picturing the lonely places of the earth — the seashore, the mountains, the Great Lakes — his landscapes with their feeling for space and light had an undertone of reserved but penetrating emotion, a serene melancholy. And always they retained a sense of the structure of the earth, its bare backbone of rocks and hills.

The Barbizon school was the first French movement to have a definite influence in the United States. Curiously enough, French romanticism, which had preceded it, found little response until the 1860's, notably through John La Farge. Even the Barbizon influence reached these shores a generation late — a time-lag typical of nineteenth-century America. But from then on, the former dominant British influence (and the more limited but important influence of Italy) were to give way more and more to that of France.

From the 1850's on a number of Americans lived and worked in the village of Barbizon. William Morris Hunt became a close friend of Millet's, and on returning to America became his champion in this country. A stimulating teacher, and a gadfly to the proper Boston art world, Hunt spread the Barbizon gospel, so much at variance with established ideas. In his own work Millet's influence was superimposed on an innate breadth of vision. For some years, his was a voice crying in the wilderness, but eventually the Barbizon influence was to prove the most decisive up to this time. Hunt's pioneering, together with that of Inness, marked the beginning of the end of literal romanticism of the Hudson River type, and the birth of a new kind of subjective romanticism.

Hunt was also a pioneer in mural painting. His two large murals executed in 1878 for the New York State Capitol in Albany, for which *Anahita* was one of the studies, and the murals of his friend and pupil John La Farge, were the first progressive notes in American mural art.

The picturing of life in the United States, initiated by the native genre painters, was brought to maturity by Winslow Homer and Thomas Eakins. These two can be considered the leading American representatives of the worldwide movement of naturalism, the realistic picturing of the contemporary scene. Compared to their predecessors they were more mature artists, franker in their realism, broader and deeper in content. Homer as a young man painted rural

America, favorite theme of the older school, with a fresher, bolder vision, and an unsentimental poetry. His early pictures of summer resort and farm, of childhood and outdoor life, were the most authentic expression of American country life in the 1860's and 1870's. From the first he painted by eye more than by tradition; his direct, candid statement of what he saw was curiously similar to the current style of the young French impressionists, but without any direct influence from them. He was an independent American pioneer of the impressionist vision.

In middle life Homer settled in a lonely spot on the Maine coast. Here his art reached full development. He was now concerned with the elemental in nature and mankind: the sea, the forest, the mountains, and the hardy men who inhabited them — sailors, fishermen, woodsmen. He became a pictorial poet of outdoor life in America, of the pioneer spirit that survived in those who lived close to nature. In his great marines he expressed, as few modern artists have, the power, the drama and the dangerous beauty of the sea. The vitality of his mature work, its perennial freshness of vision, largeness of form, resonant color harmonies, and superb decorative values, rank it among the highest artistic achievements of the period.

By contrast with Homer, Eakins took the ordinary middle-class city life of his time and place, and with uncompromising realism built his art out of this intractable material. Aside from four years' study in Paris and Spain, his whole life was spent in his native city, Philadelphia; and all his subjects were drawn from his community and its people. His earliest paintings revealed a strong, original mind dealing directly with realities. Eakins was an unusual combination of artist and scientist: a mathematician, an anatomist, and a great teacher. His whole art was based on form; it was sculptural and completely three-dimensional.

But such austere virtues were not designed for popularity. His pictures found few buyers. His insistence on the complete nude in teaching anatomy resulted in the loss of his position as head of the Pennsylvania Academy school. In middle life he abandoned his earlier picturing of the contemporary scene, and concentrated on portraiture. His portraits had a strength of character, a psychological penetration and an inner vitality, that made him the most profound American portraitist of the century. Though failing completely in worldly success, he nevertheless created the most solid and revealing record of the American people of his time — equal to Copley's record of colonial America.

Eakins was meant to be a great painter of the human body. But the prudery of his environment, combined with his own unwavering realism, thwarted his full development in this direction. In a few compositions in which the nude figure was the central motif, such as *The Swimming Hole,* he revealed potentialities as a plastic designer beyond any contemporary American except his exact opposite, Albert Ryder.

The American mind is generally regarded as practical, materialistic and extroverted. All this is undoubtedly true of one side of the national character and culture. But equally characteristic, if less frequent, is romanticism, which has been a constant element in American art since the days of West and Allston. In Cole and the Hudson River school it had taken the form of an external romanticism of subject-matter. With Inness and Hunt it had become more subjective. Earlier still, William Page, a brilliant mind akin to Allston's, and like him steeped in Italy, antiquity and the Renaissance, had created an individual romantic art based on ancient sculpture and Venetian color, yet filled with a grave personal poetry, as in his remarkable portraits of himself and his wife.

Robert Loftin Newman's romanticism was stimulated by contact with Millet at Barbizon in the 1850's. His Biblical and legendary paintings, while related to Delacroix and Diaz, were quite individual — often fragmentary, but deep in their somber brooding poetry. With George Fuller, on the other hand, romanticism was a native product of long isolated years on his Massachusetts farm, where he evolved an introspective art in which evocative figures of women inhabit a twilit autumnal world. These painters were counterparts of such writers as Hawthorne and Melville, Poe and Emily Dickinson.

But the most original romantic of the period was Albert Ryder. Born and brought up in the old whaling port of New Bedford, Ryder throughout his life was haunted by the sea. His art had no relation to things around him; he was a visionary, living in a world of poetry and legend, of imaginary landscapes and seascapes. Often he drew on the great poetic literature of the world, especially Shakespeare. But all his themes were transformed by a personal alchemy into completely original imagery. As with all genuine mystics, Ryder's inner world carries the conviction of intense, haunting reality.

His style was as personal as his content. In his works all the dead wood of his romantic predecessors was eliminated

— the nostalgia for the Old World that had enfeebled Allston, the literalism that had encumbered the Hudson River painters. He once said: "The artist should fear to become the slave of detail. He should express his thought and not the surface of it. What avails a storm-cloud accurate in form and color if the storm is not therein?" He used natural forms with great freedom, shaping them to his own conceptions. The originality and inner life of his forms, his sense of pictorial rhythm, the depth and richness of his color, and above all, his sense of design, ranked him among the purest plastic creators of his time in any country. His art was strangely prophetic of certain tendencies of our day — our discovery of the subconscious mind, our repudiation of literal naturalism, our free use of form and color to produce abstract design. When one follows the rhythms of *Jonah*, one understands why Jackson Pollock felt a particular affinity to Ryder.

As Ryder was haunted by the sea, Ralph Blakelock was haunted by the forest, the primeval background of America, with its Indian inhabitants, its mystery and terror — the old obsession with the wilderness, but now in a subjective vein. Without Ryder's full range of imagination, Blakelock was primarily a landscapist. Like Ryder's, his world was usually a nocturnal one. He loved to silhouette masses of foliage against the moonlit sky, to drop veils of mist between foreground and distance, to create patterns of receding planes, suggestive of Japanese art.

Homer, Eakins and Ryder lived most of their years in their native land, and drew their material from American life or the inner life of the mind. With contemporary European movements, which were evolving from impressionism to post-impressionism, they had little or no connection. In relation to European trends they were definitely anachronistic. Yet they were among the most creative American artists of their period, and the closest to us today. Many of the strongest nineteenth-century Americans were relatively isolated figures, playing little part in innovating world movements. Such innovations came largely from abroad, transmitted by more impressionable personalities. Here again we see the two main forces that have shaped American art: native creativity, which with all its limitations was the root of the whole tree; and the fertilizing influence of new ideas and knowledge without which no art can continue to grow. We can take Homer, Eakins and Ryder as outstanding examples of the first force, and Hunt and Inness of the second.

Another leading representative of the second type, the artist who acts as a leavening agent, was John La Farge. The most cultivated American artist of his generation, he was a many-sided personality: critic, muralist, designer of stained glass, student of the old masters. In all his work one is aware of a mind richly stored with the great traditions of art, yet unexpectedly open to new visual discoveries. His style stemmed from the Venetians and Delacroix, but his early interest in problems of outdoor color anticipated impressionism. The romantic richness of his color was modified by exotic notes from the Far East, derived from lifelong study of Oriental art and from two long visits to Japan and the South Pacific. While a highly intelligent traditionalist more than a powerful creator, La Farge played an essential role in the artistic maturing of his country.

With all his internationalism, La Farge's career was identified with the United States. But as cosmopolitanism increased, a growing number of Americans spent most of their lives in Europe, including three of the leading figures of the period: James McNeill Whistler, John S. Sargent and Mary Cassatt.

Whistler, born in America and passing most of his childhood and youth there, was thereafter a complete cosmopolite, living most of his life in London. As a young man in Paris he imbibed the naturalism of the mid-century with its rejection of so-called "literary" subjects, and he shared in the discovery of Velázquez and Goya, and of Japanese art. A conscious theorist, highly articulate, Whistler realized clearly that art is not imitation of nature but her transformation into visual design. The subject became a motif for composition almost as abstract as music. His gift was primarily decorative rather than structural: an extreme sensitivity to tonal, chromatic and spatial values and the patterns they created. To achieve his harmonies he simplified forms, muted colors, and spread veils of delicate silvery grays — just as twilight and night, his favorite hours, mute and unify the visible world. Though his art fell short of the vitality of Velázquez or of his own contemporaries Manet and Degas, within its deliberately imposed limits everything in it was essential and pure. Through both his art and his pronouncements, in spite of ridicule, Whistler helped to purge nineteenth-century painting of story-telling and photographic representation. His influence throughout the English-speaking world was wide, and played an important role in the evolution from literal naturalism toward the abstract art of our day.

In the last third of the century Paris became the Mecca of most American students. But for a time in the 1870's Munich was a close rival. Here Wilhelm Leibl and his pupils had revived the bravura of Hals and Velázquez. It was a limited discipline, concentrating on painting the model with a fresh eye and a bold brush. The old technique of drawing, underpainting and successive overpaintings gave way to direct painting. Several Americans took part in the movement, including Frank Duveneck, Walter Shirlaw, J. Frank Currier and William M. Chase. The most dynamic was Duveneck, in whose hands the new technique became a thing of beauty in itself, a rich sensuous creation within a narrow range. But his vitality was short-lived; after his return to America in 1888 his art deteriorated sadly.

Of all the Munich group Chase was the most versatile, ranging from Whistlerian decorativeness to the open-air vision of impressionism. He painted many aspects of contemporary America, indoors and outdoors, with zest, charm and delightful freshness of eye and hand. His landscapes of his beloved Long Island, combining idyllicism with keen observation, were filled with the happiness of summer, sunlight and the sea.

The new style of direct painting had one of its most brilliant cosmopolitan exponents in John Singer Sargent. Born in Italy of American parents, he received a thorough academic training in Paris, settled in London at twenty-eight, and soon had an international reputation. At the height of his career Sargent was the most sought-after portraitist in the Anglo-American world, with a waiting-list of the eminent and wealthy. His sitters were far different from Eakins' middle-class professionals and intellectuals; they were the upper crust, in all their glory. And he gave them the full treatment. Sargent belonged in the great worldly tradition of British portraiture, enjoying the spectacle of beauty, fashion and luxury, and knowing how to extract from them the maximum pictorial effect.

The central fact in Sargent's art was his extraordinary skill with the brush. His brushwork was a virtuoso performance which, like that of a brilliant pianist, gives its own kind of enjoyment. On the other hand, his standard portraits were not notable for human warmth or powerful realization of character such as Eakins had. By comparison, Sargent's art was deficient in substance and plasticity, concerned with what meets the eye rather than fundamental form and design. But as a portraitist in the grand style he was a worthy successor to Romney and Lawrence. And frequently we find a different Sargent, painting a man or woman who interested him, or delightful informal pictures of his friends; and we wish that this gifted man had been a less successful portraitist and more often purely a painter.

Meanwhile in France impressionism was in full course. Outdoor light and color, atmosphere and changing visual effects had become the new interests. An early member of the movement was the American-born Mary Cassatt, who had settled in France in her early twenties, become a friend of Degas, and at his invitation had exhibited with the impressionist group from 1879 on. Mary Cassatt, however, was never an orthodox impressionist. The influence of Degas with his insistence on precise draftsmanship outweighed the new tendency to dissolve forms in light and atmosphere. She remained characteristically American in her adherence to a naturalistic vision, and in the simplicity and wholesomeness of her favorite theme, women with their children — a completely feminine, matriarchal world. French art with its rational sensuality, its constant awareness of sex, its unending search for new forms, never affected her fundamentally. Through all her lifetime in France she remained a downright American spinster, who kept on painting the themes that meant most to her in a style of crystalline clarity and quiet strength.

In the United States there had been several native precursors of impressionism, notably Homer and La Farge. But the actual French movement, fully developed by 1870, had little direct impact here until fifteen or twenty years later. The four pioneers of American impressionism came to the movement gradually and by different paths. The earliest, Theodore Robinson, did not discover Monet until 1884, when he went to Giverny and worked in direct touch with the master (as Hunt had with Millet thirty years before). Though the influence of Monet was obvious, Robinson was a sensitive artist who saw nature freshly and with a sure instinct for color. His early death prevented full realization of his gifts.

J. Alden Weir, who had studied in Paris as early as 1873, by about 1890 had evolved a modified impressionism, exchanging his early dark palette for a higher-keyed one of reserved silvery tones, avoiding the full brilliancy of the new school. A figure painter as well as a landscapist, Weir was a more conscious designer than his fellows.

John Twachtman's impressionism was a product of personal growth more than external influence. A lyrical painter, subtle and highly sensitive, he loved the fluid and evanescent in nature: flowing water, the tenderness of early spring, snow with its white and gray world. Freer than his colleagues from a naturalistic vision, he created an art which was pure emotional expression in color, tone and space — a form of visual music. With all his seeming vagueness and fragility, his work was based on drawing and definite pattern. In all this he was a precursor of such early modernists as Prendergast and Marin.

Of the four, the closest to French impressionism was the youngest, Childe Hassam, with his love of full sunlight and his use of the new technique of divided tones. A fresh observer with a wide range of subjects, he delighted equally in the gay spectacle of the streets of Paris and New York, the trim white-painted villages of New England, and the blue sea and soft air of American summer resorts. In its enjoyment of the pleasant aspects of life, Hassam's work was one of the happiest creations of American impressionism.

For American art impressionism opened up a new world of light and color, air and sunshine. Coinciding with the increasing physical freedom of the American people and their growing love of outdoor life, impressionism eventually had the widest influence of any European movement so far. Transplanted to the United States, it was modified by American naturalism and sentiment to produce an idyllic art quite different from the earthiness of Renoir and Monet. The solid actualities of nature were less important than the light that fell on them and the atmosphere that enveloped them. Subjects became even more informal than with Inness and Martin — intimate corners of nature. The favorite painting ground was the relatively long-settled East, with its seaside resorts and charming old villages. The love of the spacious and spectacular aspects of America that had inspired the Hudson River painters was a thing of the past.

At the turn of the century American art had reached a pause in its development. The earlier leaders — Inness, La Farge, Homer, Eakins, Ryder — were either dead or well on in years. The younger generation had a different background. Most of them had studied in the academic schools of Paris, and they were apt to be less adventurous than their elders had been, more inclined to accept the limited tradition of the Salon. More cosmopolitan, they were not interested in the American scene; after France, the United States must have seemed raw and ugly. They were men of refinement more than power, lacking Homer's or Eakins' ability to extract

artistic content out of the crude ore of American life. They avoided the vulgar actualities of the common life, and devoted themselves to the environment and ideals of the upper and middle classes. Their art centered around the family and home, the healthy and pleasant aspects of society, and the idyllic in nature.

Women played a central role in much of their art. Never in our previous history had painters and sculptors concentrated so much on the feminine. With the idealism that was so deeply ingrained in the nineteenth-century American mind, they pictured woman as a being finer and purer than the male, not only more beautiful physically but representing ideals of spiritual beauty. She appeared in many roles: as the young mother with her children, as the housewife in her sheltered home, as the allegorical figure symbolizing abstract virtues, and as the maiden still untouched by life, embodying the cult of virginity that was so marked in American culture of the time.

This idealistic devotion to womanhood achieved full expression with Abbott Thayer. His entire art was given to ideals of bodily and spiritual beauty incarnated in female form. His women had the air of angels or goddesses, combining strength, generosity, candor and innocence. There was a genuine nobility in them, and a grave serenity. Thayer's style had a large simplicity, a sensuous handling of pigment, and resonant color, never oversweet as with so many of his colleagues. His art was American traditionalism in its most affirmative aspect.

Similar ideals were expressed in George de Forest Brush's favorite image of a mother with her children, pictured in a style close to the Pre-Raphaelites in its reminiscences of fifteenth-century Italy, and in its flowing lines and meticulous attention to detail. With Thomas W. Dewing the recurring theme was again womankind. His ethereal creatures, extravagantly leisured, sit in shadowy rooms remote from the turmoil of the outside world, in a rarified atmosphere of emptiness and silence and waiting; or outdoors in the twilight they stand rapt, listening to the nightingale or to one of their number reciting or playing a violin. The occasional absurdity of these fantasies is somehow captivating; they are exquisite sonnets to femininity. Their creation of a dreamlike world, half real and half visionary, was a foretaste of surrealism.

The chief artistic limitation of these traditionalists, like that of their predecessors of the mid-century, was their concept of art as literal representation, instead of free creation in form and color. But their art had its positive virtues, not only as the expression of a prevailing culture, but in its more purely artistic qualities: technical skill, sound draftsmanship, refinements of color and tone, and pleasure in handling the brush. Such qualities have perennial value, regardless of changes in taste.

American sculpture throughout the nineteenth century was more solidly conservative than painting. Professionalism had developed later, and sculpture was still dominated by the historic past, and specifically the Greco-Roman tradition. And there was the factor of official standards. Painting had many private uses and patrons, and painters could express themselves with greater freedom and individualism. Sculptors, on the other hand, depended considerably on public commissions: outdoor monuments, sculptured portraits of the great, and architectural decoration. Official taste was by its nature conservative, particularly in a democracy where every citizen had the right to admire or condemn. So public opinion affected the sculptor more directly than the painter.

The age of monuments had begun in the 1830's. Every city of any size had to have its bronze equestrian figure of George Washington. The chief virtue of such works was as patriotic images for the people and as decoration for parks, but they did evidence a growing recognition of art as a legitimate concern of governments, whether federal, state or local. And by and large, monumental sculpture exhibited more vitality than Italianate neo-classicism. Dealing with the actualities of American history, it was freer from neo-classic formulas and sentimentality. For example, Clark Mills, who had never been abroad, and in fact had only recently seen an actual piece of sculpture by anyone but himself, produced in his Andrew Jackson for Lafayette Square in Washington — Old Hickory on a prancing horse, doffing his hat — a work which with all its naive and comic aspects possessed genuine vigor. Henry Kirke Brown, one of the first to maintain that study in Italy was not essential, created in his equestrian George Washington for Union Square, New York, an image that is still impressive.

After 1860 the prestige of Rome as a center for study gave way to that of Paris, where current creation was livelier and where the Ecole des Beaux-Arts offered the most rigorous and thorough academic training of the time. And with the 1880's came the more vital influence of Rodin, which affected most American sculptors in varying degrees for the next thirty years. The stale neo-classicism of Italy was replaced by increasing range of subject-matter, a more naturalistic view-

point, and much greater technical command. But conservatism still predominated; the gain was in skill and versatility more than originality. Accomplished naturalism remained the criterion, rather than plastic creation. There were no sculptor counterparts to Whistler, Homer, Eakins, Ryder, or the impressionist painters.

By the 1890's the accumulation of national wealth, the nation's expanding role as a world power, and the new scale and ostentation of American life resulted in a wide public building program that spread throughout the country the Beaux-Arts style in architecture, sculpture and mural painting. The lavish decorations of the Chicago World's Fair of 1893 ushered in the golden age of academic American sculpture and mural art. In this expansion of public art, sculpture on the whole produced the most solid achievements. American mural painting was still in its infancy, and most of its works, with a few honorable exceptions such as La Farge, Thayer and Elihu Vedder, were enlarged easel paintings. But sculptors by the nature of their medium had to consider physical materials and substance, and relations to architecture and setting. Monumental sculpture remained academic until the 1930's, and produced its real horrors, rivalling the worst of the French Beaux-Arts school. But it also produced Augustus Saint-Gaudens, a complete traditionalist who transcended the limitations of his school. No major artist was closer to the norm of the nineteenth-century American mind — the desire, as he said, to combine "the real with the ideal." In his work native idealism was united with native naturalism in a balanced amalgam. Nobility of subject and spirit were matched by vital energy. His figures were alive with movement: the marching rhythm of the Negro soldiers in the Shaw memorial, the triumphant progress of General Sherman with his attendant winged Victory. In Saint-Gaudens' art American traditionalism reached its fullest and finest expression.

HOMER D. MARTIN: *The Iron Mine, Port Henry, New York.*
Oil. 30 x 50.
National Collection of Fine Arts, Smithsonian Institution.

GEORGE INNESS: *Early Morning, Tarpon Springs.*
1892. Oil. 42 x 32¼.
The Art Institute of Chicago.

GEORGE INNESS: *The Monk.*
1873. Oil. 39½ x 64.
Addison Gallery of American Art.

WILLIAM PAGE: *Self Portrait*.
c. 1860. Oil. 59 x 36.
The Detroit Institute of Arts.

WILLIAM PAGE: *Mrs. William Page*.
c. 1860. Oil. 60¼ x 36¼.
The Detroit Institute of Arts.

WILLIAM MORRIS HUNT: *Anahita, or The Flight of Night.*
1878. Oil. 62⅝ x 95¼.
Museum of Fine Arts, Boston.

ALBERT P. RYDER: *The Flying Dutchman*.
c. 1887. Oil. 13¾ x 16½.
National Collection of Fine Arts, Smithsonian Institution.

ALBERT P. RYDER: *The Race Track.*
1890-1910. Oil. 28¼ x 35¼.
The Cleveland Museum of Art.

RALPH ALBERT BLAKELOCK: *Ecstasy.*
Oil. 30 x 38.
The Hackley Art Gallery.

EASTMAN JOHNSON: *Sugaring-off, Number 2.*
1865-1875. Oil. 33 x 54.
The Butler Institute of American Art.

JAMES A. MCNEILL WHISTLER: *Wapping on Thames.*
1861. Oil. 28 x 40.
Collection of Mr. and Mrs. John Hay Whitney.

JAMES A. MCNEILL WHISTLER: *Lady of the Lange Lijsen.*
1864. Oil. 36¼ x 24¼.
John G. Johnson Collection.

JOHN SINGER SARGENT: *Mme. Edouard Pailleron.*
1879. Oil. 82 x 39½.
The Corcoran Gallery of Art.

FRANK DUVENECK: *Amy Folsom*.
c. 1880. Oil. 36 x 23¾.
The Montclair Art Museum.

WINSLOW HOMER: *The Fox Hunt.*
1893. Oil. 38 x 68.
Pennsylvania Academy of the Fine Arts.

WINSLOW HOMER: *West Point, Prout's Neck.*
1900. Oil. 30 x 48.
Sterling and Francine Clark Art Institute.

THEODORE ROBINSON: *On the Towpath — A Halt*
1893-1894. Oil. 28 x 40.
Collection of Mr. and Mrs. Cornelius Vanderbilt Whitney.

MARY CASSATT: *Young Women Picking Fruit.*
1891. Oil. 51¼ x 35¾.
Museum of Art, Carnegie Institute.

MARY CASSATT: *The Bath.*
c. 1891-1892. Oil. 39½ x 26.
The Art Institute of Chicago.

THOMAS EAKINS: *Miss Van Buren.*
c. 1889-91. Oil. 45 x 32.
The Phillips Collection.

THOMAS EAKINS: *The Swimming Hole.*
1883. Oil. 27 x 36.
Fort Worth Art Association.

THOMAS W. DEWING: *The Recitation.*
1891. Oil. 30 x 55.
The Detroit Institute of Arts.

WILLIAM M. CHASE: *Hide and Seek.*
1888. Oil. 27½ x 36.
The Phillips Collection.

JOHN H. TWACHTMAN: *Azaleas.*
c. 1898. Oil. 30 x 24.
Randolph-Macon Woman's College.

JOHN SINGER SARGENT: *Group with Parasols*.
Probably 1908 or 1910. Oil. 21 x 27¾.
Collection of Rita and Daniel Fraad.

CHILDE HASSAM: *The Summer Girl.*
1894. Oil. 32 x 32.
Collection of Mr. and Mrs. Ogden Phipps.

AUGUSTUS SAINT-GAUDENS: *Diana.*
1892. Gilded bronze. 112 high.
The Metropolitan Museum of Art.

4 Modernism and the American Scene

As the twentieth century opened, the American art world was a peaceful one, completely dominated by the traditionalists. The last movement to reach these shores had been impressionism; of European developments since then the established order remained unaware. But this peaceful scene was about to be invaded by two forces: a new realism, and the modern movements from abroad. Within a quarter century these two were to effect more fundamental changes in American art than in all the preceding centuries.

The first invasion was by a group of young realist painters: Robert Henri (the oldest and the leader), George Luks, William J. Glackens, John Sloan and Everett Shinn. All five were Philadelphians and close friends, and all but Henri had begun as newspaper artists. In revolt against academic idealism they turned for subjects to the contemporary city — at first Philadelphia, then New York — its people, streets, theaters, restaurants and dancehalls, the glamor of its night life, its infinite variety of character and incident. Relishing low life as much as high life, they pictured the city and its people with warm humanity, and with a humor that had been sadly lacking in American art for years. Their work had the first-hand contact with actualities, the authentic flavor and the vitality of the best genre art of all countries and periods.

All of them were in revolt against impressionism; or rather, what impressionism had become in America. Instead they looked back to the great seventeenth-century naturalists Velázquez, Hals and Rembrandt, and their modern descendants Goya, Daumier and Manet. All of the five were gifted draftsmen, and their painting style combined graphic vividness with breadth. Their dark early color was a reaction against academic sweetness and light. They were far from radical compared to current European developments; it was their realistic subject-matter that made them seem radical to the established art world, which labelled them "Apostles of Ugliness."

Abroad, meanwhile, revolutionary movements were taking place. In France the post-impressionists and neo-impressionists, rejecting impressionism's visual naturalism, had re-created reality in terms of fundamental form. Now, in the early 1900's, Matisse and the fauves were using reality as only a starting-point for free creation, in which color, line and design became a direct physical language. Figures and objects, freely distorted, were translated into powerful rhythmic patterns. Color was raised to a new purity and intensity. Then in 1908 cubism was born: an exploration of three-dimensional volumes instead of fauvism's emphasis on color and pattern. The object was broken down into its geometric components, reassembled in new combinations, seen from different sides simultaneously. Cubism's radical experiments gave birth to other innovations, including the beginnings of pure abstraction. In these years Paris was the center of new movements, crowding one upon another, that revolutionized the basic concepts of art.

In these developments more than a score of Americans participated. As early as the 1890's Maurice Prendergast had discovered Cézanne and Bonnard, and had begun to evolve his personal lyrical and decorative art, in which nature was transformed into enchanting arabesques of line and color. Prendergast can be called the first American modernist — the first to paint pictures which were independent creations in line and color and rhythmic pattern.

After 1900 more young artists arrived in Paris and came into contact with modernism. Never before had so many Americans been involved so early in an international movement. Mostly in their twenties, they had seen little or no modern art back home, and it was bewildering at first. For almost all, Cézanne was the first and most lasting influence. Matisse and the fauves were more comprehensible than Picasso and the cubists. With some exceptions, their own work abroad was not radical, and only after returning home did they develop more advanced styles.

A few remained outside the Parisian orbit: Marsden Hartley in Germany, where he became allied with expressionism; Joseph Stella in Italy and later in Paris, in contact with Italian futurism; and Maurice Sterne in the Orient, including two years in Bali, where he painted the dark passionate life of the tropics. Some Americans lived abroad for years and were integral members of the European art world, such as Lyonel Feininger, who became a leader of German modernism. On the other hand, some future modernists spent years abroad without being influenced by current movements: John Marin and Arthur Dove, both complete individualists, were to have their first real introduction to modern art through Alfred Stieglitz in New York. But in most cases it was European and usually French modernism that furnished the first great stimulus.

When the young pioneers of modern art came home, they found a very different artistic climate. The United States' phenomenal material growth had not been matched by artistic growth. The art world was under complete conservative control. The big national exhibitions, the only means for a young or unknown artist to reach the public, were dominated by academic juries who excluded anyone of independent tendencies. But this academic domination was being challenged by the young realists of the Henri group, doughty fighters for artistic independence. Soon they became allied with three other painters, of different viewpoints but similar liberal beliefs: Prendergast, Arthur B. Davies and Ernest Lawson. The group, which came to be called "The Eight," staged a series of exhibitions, including an historic show at the Macbeth Gallery in 1908. In the next few years they were joined by other young liberals and modernists in organizing large independent exhibitions, culminating in the great Armory Show of 1913, which introduced modern art to a bewildered, shocked but enormously curious American public. No international movement had ever before been launched in this way in the United States. In the past there had always been a time-lag of fifteen or twenty years before European movements reached us. But within eight years of the birth of fauvism and five years of that of cubism, the Armory Show presented a panorama of the Parisian art scene, including the latest developments such as Marcel Duchamp's *Nude Descending a Staircase*. No single event, before or since, has had such an influence on American art.

As the modern movements evolved in the United States after the Armory Show, they produced fewer radical innovations than in Europe. To the Europeans, the resources of representational art appeared to be exhausted, and the only possible path was the creation of a new artistic language. But American art had not yet reached this stage of evolution; up to 1913 it had been almost completely representational.

Some abstract art had been produced before 1913; but the Armory Show gave a strong impetus to abstraction, and for the next decade it was practised by a dozen Americans. They formed no school; their styles were personal. Most of their work was semi-abstract rather than pure abstract. Compared to the Europeans, they were concerned less with formal problems than with emotional expression. Cubism had a few exponents, especially Max Weber, Andrew Dasburg and William Zorach. But even Weber, its most inventive practitioner, was unorthodox. His interpretations of New York such as *Chinese Restaurant* were partly cubistic in style, but their rapturous response to the spectacle of the modern city was closer to futurism. In general, early American abstraction tended to be expressionist rather than formal. Often it showed an affinity to Kandinsky's free-form abstraction. In Germany between 1912 and 1915 Marsden Hartley, affiliated with the *Blaue Reiter* group of whom Kandinsky was a leader, painted bold abstract compositions, powerful in their primary colors, superb in decorative pattern.

Several Americans who remained abroad were involved in European abstract movements. The most eminent, Lyonel Feininger, in 1912 evolved a cubistic style with parallels to futurism in its dynamic thrust and counter-thrust. Feininger himself said that his lifelong love of ships, locomotives and tall buildings had begun in his childhood and youth in New York.

In Paris in 1913 Morgan Russell and Stanton Macdonald-Wright launched their own abstract movement, Synchromism — meaning "with color" — a rival to the Orphism of Robert Delaunay. The two Americans, both intelligent theorists, based their aesthetic on the fact that the warm colors appear to advance toward the eye, while the cool colors retreat; and that these sensations of projection and recession could be used to create pictorial space and form. The Synchromists' early compositions were much like their rivals', multi-colored prisms and whirling disks; but in the next few years they developed more complex and interesting designs. Though they evolved a method rather than a content, their analysis of color-form relations was a contribution to abstract theory.

Back in the United States, indigenous abstraction appeared in Arthur G. Dove and Georgia O'Keeffe. Dove's art was close to the earth; its motifs, based on nature, were transformed into strong rhythmic patterns and resonant color harmonies. Georgia O'Keeffe's art from the first was a personal language without discernible derivations, at times attaining abstraction as pure as music. Her design was daring and effective, her style crystal-clear — yet always with a sense of dark enigmatic depths beneath the brilliant surface.

The first American abstract movement lasted only until about 1920. After that most of its exponents turned to more representational styles. Abstraction was not, as in Europe, the end product of long historical evolution. It had no roots in the American past. Our art world, barely emerged from impressionism, was not prepared for so complete a break with tradition. From 1920 until the mid-1930's only a few Americans worked in abstract terms, and even they not exclusively: Dove, O'Keeffe, Arthur B. Carles, Stuart Davis, Patrick Henry Bruce in Paris, and younger men such as Gorky and the sculptors Calder and Noguchi.

The United States of 1913, building its early skyscrapers and airplanes, could be called the most futurist nation. But its dynamism had produced no echo in academic art. The machine age had found a voice in Italian futurism, Russian constructivism, and French and Spanish cubism, but not so far in American art. Our most spectacular city, New York, had been painted by a few impressionists and the romantic realists of the Henri group, who had focussed on its human aspects. But about 1912 the city itself — its towering buildings, soaring bridges and rushing traffic, and the kaleidoscope of its night lights — became themes for modernists such as Marin, Weber, Walkowitz and Stella. Interpreting the city in semi-abstract terms, they were the first to express in non-representational style the essential energies of machine-age America.

Orthodox futurism, however, found little following here. Launched in Italy in 1910, it was a glorification of the machine, speed and dynamism — a doctrine one might expect to appeal especially to Americans. Yet the school had only one out-and-out American representative, Joseph Stella. Born in Italy, living in the United States since youth, he met the Italian futurists in Paris in 1912. Soon after the Armory Show he embarked on a series of large futurist fantasies based on New York — still among the most imaginative visions of the modern city.

Though cubism, like futurism, had only a few adherents, its influence was much wider than its practice. Its concentration on form, its geometric style and precision, affected artists who did not follow it all the way into abstraction. In particular the painters who have been called precisionists profited by its lessons. These men used the phenomena of urban and industrial America — skyscrapers, factories, railroads, machine-made objects — as raw material. Though more or less representational, they were interested primarily in the geometric forms of such things, and in translating them into precise ordered design.

Charles Demuth, picturing the monuments of industry in a personal variation of cubism, created an inventive play with the geometric, and achieved pure design that combined refinement and a classic sense of order. Morton Schamberg was one of the first Americans to explore the aesthetic possibilities of the machine itself, transforming its functional shapes into clear and finely organized semi-abstract design. A gifted artist, his promise was cut short by his early death.

Of all the precisionists Charles Sheeler realized most completely the aesthetics of the machine age. In the machine and its products he found a functional purity that lent itself perfectly to formal presentation. After early experiments with abstraction he evolved a completely realistic style of extreme, often photographic exactness, but always built on a structure of geometric form. In later years Sheeler returned to semi-abstraction, with added complexity and technical mastery.

Precision had been one characteristic of much American painting from the beginning. But the origin of modern precisionism was cubism's exploration of basic form in the 1910's. Paradoxically, Parisian cubism, by stimulating the precisionists to throw off impressionist softness and vagueness, helped them to return to the clarity that had marked precise realism in America from the time of the limners, and of Feke and Copley.

By far the most widespread form of American modernism until the middle 1930's was expressionism. The word is a broad and rather indefinite one, but the only one to cover one of the widest tendencies in modern art. It had been first applied to the German modern schools such as *Die Brücke* and *Der Blaue Reiter,* which reacting against impressionism's focus on the merely visual, turned to expression of subjective emotion. With time the word came to include the many artists, neither naturalistic on the one hand nor abstract on the other, who aimed to express emotion through imagery based on reality, but not realistically represented. The expressionist drew on nature for images, but used them freely, in a style that tended toward semi-abstraction. Through rhythmic line, richness of material, and above all through color, expressionism spoke to the senses, and through the senses to the emotions.

Expressionism proved particularly sympathetic to the American mind, which has never been as attracted to formal qualities as to emotional expression based on reality. It was the most widely practised mode among our pioneer modernists, and the mode to which those who abandoned abstraction usually turned. Its currency can be ascribed in part to the emergence of many modernists of central and eastern European origin. Since the German expressionists were only scantily represented in the Armory Show, and in the American art world for a decade after, it seems evident that expressionism was less a product of foreign influence than a parallel development — a characteristic creation of the new America.

Expressionism was not so much a school as a broad tendency, highly diverse, with as many variations as individuals. To cite only a few: John Marin, with his lyrical interpretations of the electric vitality of New York or the vibrant light of the Maine coast. A born colorist, sometimes delicate, sometimes magnificently rich; a graphic master whose line was charged with life; and an intuitive designer whose most spontaneous watercolors had a quality of inevitability —

Marin was one of the purest creative artists of his time. Or Marsden Hartley, whose early mountain landscapes with their visionary strangeness revealed his youthful admiration for Albert Ryder. After years of cosmopolitanism and abstract experimentation, Hartley returned to his native Maine and painted its seacoast and mountains with an elemental simplicity like that of his early work, but with greater power. Or Max Weber's art after he gave up abstraction: idyllic and religious themes, Biblical in spirit, expressive of serene contemplation or spiritual exaltation. Many other Americans could be numbered among the expressionists. To the sterility of established art expressionism brought a new emotional freedom, a new sensuousness, and a more direct and powerful visual language.

American sculpture was affected by modernism much later and less than painting. In the opening years of the century it was almost completely conservative: a proficient academic neo-classicism, coldly idealized, and limited to naturalistic representation, a kind of three-dimensional photography. The historical traditionalism of our sculptors compared to our painters held true well into the new century. There were few counterparts to the fauvist, cubist and expressionist painters. Public commissions went to the academicians; and there were practical problems: the nature of the medium, solid and heavy, requiring much time and labor, and ample studio space. And American modernism was not much concerned with form, the basis of sculpture. A few essays were made in sculptural abstraction, such as Max Weber's small pieces of 1915 and 1917, among the earliest purely abstract sculpture produced anywhere; Robert Laurent's fluid wood carvings based on natural forms; and John Storrs' vigorous, massive constructions with their strong rhythms and clearcut planes. But these were few compared to the sculptural innovations being carried on in Europe by Brancusi, Matisse, Duchamp-Villon, Picasso, Lipchitz and many others.

When the prevailing conservatism was challenged it was by liberal rather than advanced sculptors. From the outworn neo-classic tradition these men were drawn toward primitive, archaic and non-European art, embodying other and sometimes more ancient sculptural concepts; and especially toward African Negro sculpture, a revelation of uninhibited vitality.

The style of these liberals was representational, but not naturalistic. Their most frequent theme was still the immemorial one of the human (usually the female) figure, but they used it with a new freedom. Their dominant purpose was the creation of plastic form — form alive in itself, not a copy of life. They carved no frigid marble maidens.

Gaston Lachaise's art was a hymn to the female and her sexual magnetism, incarnated in forms of the utmost amplitude and vitality, and yet of the utmost refinement: a sculptor in the great French tradition whose full creative career unfolded in this country. A similar blend of classicism and freedom marked Elie Nadelman, whose witty satires on society, with all their suavity and elegance, were highly original plastic conceptions, severely pure in form. Inventive play with the human figure was used by Hugo Robus for both humorous and serious purposes; his humor was not merely in his subjects but in his forms with their imaginative exaggerations and simplifications. William Zorach, who had begun as an expressionist painter, turned to sculpture in a style more traditional than his painting, but far from academic, marked by a monumental simplicity and a deep fullblooded sensuousness. There were Robert Laurent's later carvings in alabaster, whose translucent delicacy was a perfect medium for his feeling for material and his subtle flowing rhythms. With these artists and many others American sculpture was awakening from its long history of barren neo-classicism. In the succeeding decades it was to grow constantly in creativity and inventiveness, introducing new materials and techniques, and concepts of sculptural form and function even more revolutionary than in painting.

By the early 1920's the modern movements in the United States had begun to lose their momentum. The new decade was to bring a reaction against the internationalism of the first World War period, and a growing interest in the American scene; and then a school of social art. These successive movements were to dominate the American art world until the late 1930's. In these years little advanced art was created in this country compared to Europe.

The modernists of the 1900's and 1910's had been pioneers in hostile territory. They had introduced the new art to a nation totally unprepared for it. Neither members nor leaders of groups, they founded no schools. By and large, they were individualists, working out their artistic destinies in an unresponsive environment. As we have seen, they produced few new basic concepts, no innovations as radical as those of Matisse and Picasso. Their achievements were in the field of personal expression, in developing individual viewpoints and styles. Most of them were influenced by international modernism, but in varying ways and degrees. One can cite Marin as an example of the instinctive artist to whom modernism was a liberating atmosphere rather than a determining influence; and Weber as an example of the knowledgeable artist, responding to current developments and experimenting with them, in evolving his own mature artistic expression. In both cases it was what came from within, and what the artist made of what came from without, that counted in the end.

It was not necessarily the most advanced who made the most lasting contributions. Only a few went as far as pure abstraction; most of them maintained a base in the "real" world. But all of them shared the fundamental idea of art as free creation in the direct physical language of form, color and design, not as naturalistic representation — in which they differed completely from the academic mind.

The pioneer modernists effected a revolution in the basic concepts of the nature of art. They restored art to its basis in the senses. They purified painting and sculpture of much that was not art. Even artists who did not adopt modernism learned from it. As John Sloan said, modern art was "a medicine for the disease of imitating appearances." But modernism was not only a revolution in the language of art; it was the visual expression of a new spirit, challenging the outworn Puritanism of established American culture. It was an affirmative response to the modern world of the machine and the city. It helped to free emotional expression from genteel inhibitions, and to recognize sex as a motivating power in all human affairs. The liberating influence of international modernism added its impetus to the vast forces that were transforming the twentieth-century United States.

In the first decade of the century Henri and his fellow realists had broken the spell of academic idealism, and inaugurated a new interest in the contemporary scene. They were soon joined by other city realists: Jerome Myers, gentle poet of the slums; Glenn Coleman with his melancholy portraits of mean streets; Guy Pène du Bois with his satirical, acid glimpses of the privileged classes; and George Bellows, one of the most remarkable painting talents of his generation, who pictured the multitudinous life of the city with a technical brilliance rivalling Sargent's.

Of the same group was Edward Hopper, who as early as 1908 had painted the native scene with a new kind of realism. The Henri group had focussed on the city's human aspects, but Hopper concentrated on the modern city itself, its monumental structures, changing lights and varied visual phenomena. A work such as *Early Sunday Morning* conveyed a penetrating sense of the vastness and loneliness of the city. Hopper's paintings of the eastern countryside and small

town included all those man-made features that his idyllic predecessors had avoided: auto highways and gas stations, railroad tracks, stark New England houses. His portrayal of the twentieth-century United States was uncompromising in its honesty, yet filled with deep and poignant emotion. A poet of places more than of humanity, no artist had painted a more powerful and moving portrait of the American land and what man has made of it.

Not until the 1920's did the awakened interest in the American scene spread beyond the East. The United States west of the Alleghenies, pictured by so many nineteenth-century artists, was still an unexplored continent for most twentieth-century painters. The pioneer of the change was Charles Burchfield, who after an early phase of original romantic fantasy began about 1920 to paint the eastern Middle West: grim industrial towns, dreary streets of houses with false fronts, monstrous mansions of the President Garfield era — a record which exposed the grotesque ugliness of much of the American environment. But in all this there was much more than satire, there was a deep emotional attachment — an ambivalence of love and hate in an essentially romantic artist who had the courage to remain in his own region and to create his art out of it.

Hopper and Burchfield never intended to start a movement. The opposite was true of the regionalists Thomas H. Benton, Grant Wood and John Steuart Curry. All born and raised in the Middle West, they all studied in Europe and were exposed to modernism, but rejected it, returning to their native states. They were champions of the regionalist philosophy that there was a special virtue in an artist's identification with his own section — a virtue that was lost in cosmopolitanism. To them the Mississippi River region was the heartland of the United States, and its people and folkways had a uniquely American character. This character was to be found in the country, not in cities. So they painted the America of hillbillies, folk singers, revival meetings, windmills and limitless horizons of wheat. They cherished the oldtime virtues of this rural society, and its oldtime sins. They were not blind to its provincial and humorous aspects, and their attitudes (Wood's and Benton's in particular) had a definite element of satire — not hostile satire, but a relish for native idiosyncrasies, a blend of humor and affection. All this was combined with nostalgia; essentially romantics, they were painting an America that was already giving way to the march of standardization.

During the 1930's regionalism became a wide and active movement, stimulated partly by the governmental art projects, whose stated theme was "The American Scene." The negative aspects of the regionalist philosophy were its cultural isolationism, hostile not only to Europe but to the eastern cities, its self-consciousness, and its resistance to change in artistic ideas. But with all their limitations, the regionalists did create an authentic record of neglected aspects of American life. For the first time since the nineteenth century, the world of mid-America was painted with vitality and humor. And in purely artistic terms the best regionalist painting had qualities of substance and energy that may well make it more highly valued in the future.

Back East, a younger generation of urban realists such as Reginald Marsh, Raphael Soyer, Katherine Schmidt and Isabel Bishop were picturing New York with a realism more drastic than that of the Henri group, revealing its seamy side, the tawdriness in its glamor, its elements of poverty and misery, and the submerged life of the Bowery. Unlike Hopper's, their city was crowded with an unending procession of humanity and a babel of signs and billboards. But their basic motivation was affirmative — love of the city in its myriad aspects.

In few other countries were artists so concerned with their environment as in the United States of the 1920's and 1930's. Here was a broad land still raw and unfinished, little explored by artists, unassimilated into art — to the artist a new world, at once vital and disorderly, grand and squalid, loved and hated. The painters of the American scene dispelled the old idealistic vision of America, and achieved a visual rediscovery of the United States that paralleled the literary discoveries of Dreiser, Sherwood Anderson, Sinclair Lewis and William Faulkner.

Since the rise of capitalism and the modern state, the most creative artists have seldom been champions of the ruling forces of society. They have usually been libertarians rather than authoritarians, individualists rather than institutionalists, interested in human and democratic values more than in celebrating material power and wealth. The tremendous social and political changes of the twentieth century, shattering the seemingly secure world of the turn of the century, brought home to artists as to everyone else the fact that political and social factors directly affect all of us. The depression of the 1930's gave American artists a firsthand realization of the economic ills of society, and produced a growing trend toward the left. The rise of fascism abroad, with its suppression of cultural freedom, caused many artists to look to communism as the hope of mankind, and blinded them to its own brand of repression. Up to this time, pictorial social and political comment had been confined to cartoons and had not been expressed in the so-called fine arts, even by socialists like Sloan. But now appeared the first movement concerned primarily with social themes. Its doctrine was that art must have social content to be valid, and that mere objective, sensuous or formal representation was meaningless. Economic and social democracy, the workers' cause, and internationalism were championed; capitalism, fascism and militarism were attacked; the regionalist and American scene schools were branded as chauvinist. In orthodox social art the United States was a land of poverty, injustice, lynchings, labor massacres and dust bowls — a picture heavily weighted with Marxist clichés. In no other nation did artists say so frankly and loudly what was wrong with their country. And many of them did so while on the government's payroll during the federal art projects — a unique example of democratic freedom of expression. Artistically, the chief external influence was fortunately not the academic "social realism" of the Soviet Union, but the freer, more vital style of the Mexican revolutionary painters Rivera, Siqueiros and Orozco, all of whom executed murals in this country.

By the middle 1930's the social school was more dominant than even the rival nativist schools, especially in the large cities. Its influence, it is true, was due as much to its militant radicalism as to its actual products. The number of primarily social artists was not large, but they included such strong figures as William Gropper, Ben Shahn, Philip Evergood, George Grosz and Robert Gwathmey. The social school broadened subject-matter to include issues vital to everyone; it brought moral convictions into art, and gave satire a new edge.

By the late 1930's the regionalist, American scene and social schools were no longer active movements. Regionalism could not survive in an increasingly international world; and as to the social school, the Nazi-Soviet treaty of 1939 and the second World War made its concepts seem obsolete. But these movements, though no longer dominant, still had their individual exponents, and they had enormously enriched the range and content of American art.

WILLIAM J. GLACKENS: *Hammerstein's Roof Garden.*
c. 1901. Oil. 30 x 25.
Whitney Museum of American Art.

ERNEST LAWSON: *High Bridge.*
1934. Oil. 30 x 40.
Whitney Museum of American Art.

EORGE LUKS: *Armistice Night.*
918. Oil. 37 x 68¾.
Vhitney Museum of American Art.

JOHN SLOAN: *Backyards, Greenwich Village.*
1914. Oil. 26 x 32.
Whitney Museum of American Art.

MAURICE PRENDERGAST: *The Promenade.*
1913. Oil. 30 x 34.
Whitney Museum of American Art.

JOSEPH STELLA: *Battle of Lights, Coney Island.*
1913-1914. Oil. 75¾ x 84.
Yale University Art Gallery.

MAURICE KANTOR: *Synthetic Arrangement.*
1923. Oil. 46 x 54.
Collection of Mr. and Mrs. Arthur G. Altschul.

MARSDEN HARTLEY: *Painting. Number 5.*
1914-1915. Oil. 39½ x 31¾.
Whitney Museum of American Art.

MAN RAY: *The Rope Dancer Accompanies Herself with Her Shadows.*
1916. Oil. 52 x 73⅜.
The Museum of Modern Art.

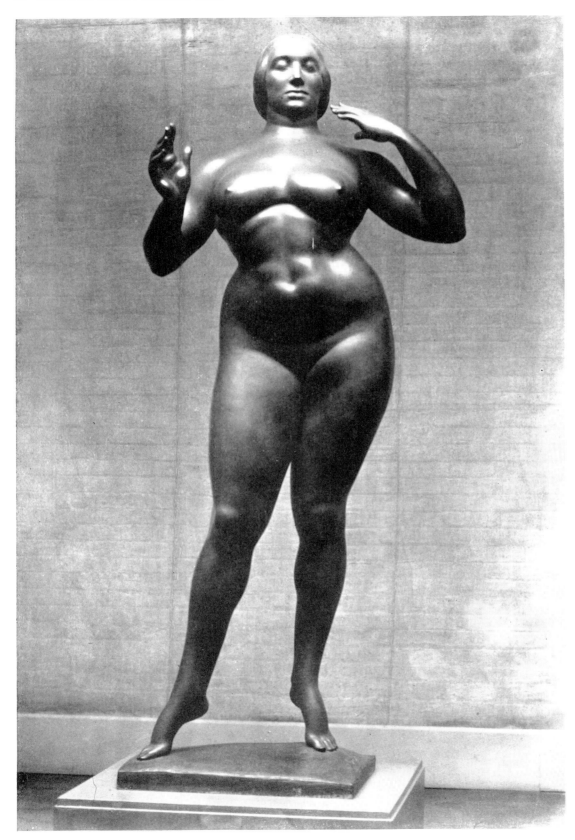

GASTON LACHAISE: *Standing Woman.*
1912-27. Bronze. 70 high.
Whitney Museum of American Art.

JOHN STORRS: *Composition Around Two Voids.*
1932. Stainless steel. 20 high.
Whitney Museum of American Art.

HUGO ROBUS: *One and Another.*
1934. Bronze. 41 long.
Sara Roby Foundation.

MAX WEBER: *Chinese Restaurant.*
1915. Oil. 40 x 48.
Whitney Museum of American Art.

JOHN MARIN: *Region of Brooklyn Bridge Fantasy.*
1932. Watercolor. 18¾ x 22¼.
Whitney Museum of American Art.

MAURICE STERNE: *Dance of the Elements.*
1913. Oil. 56¾ x 65½.
North Carolina Museum of Art.

WILLIAM ZORACH: *The Future Generation.*
1942-47. Marble. 40 high.
Whitney Museum of American Art.

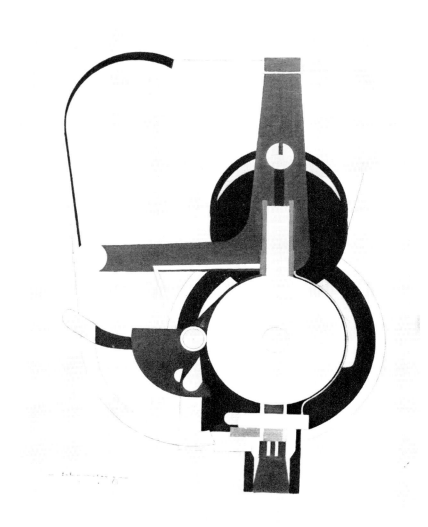

MORTON L. SCHAMBERG: *Machine.*
1916. Oil. 30⅛ x 22¾.
Yale University Art Gallery.

GEORGIA O'KEEFFE: *Abstraction.*
1926. Oil. 30 x 18.
Whitney Museum of American Art.

CHARLES DEMUTH: *My Egypt.*
1927. Oil. 35¾ x 30.
Whitney Museum of American Art.

CHARLES SHEELER: *Classic Landscape.*
1931. Oil. 25 x 32¼.
Collection of Mrs. Edsel B. Ford.

GRANT WOOD: *Stone City, Iowa.*
1930. Oil. 30¼ x 40.
Joslyn Art Museum.

THOMAS HART BENTON: *Preparing the Bill.*
1934. Oil. 46 x 38.
Randolph-Macon Woman's College.

EDWARD HOPPER: *Early Sunday Morning.*
1930. Oil. 35 x 60.
Whitney Museum of American Art.

REGINALD MARSH: *Human Pool Tables*.
1938. Egg tempera. 29¾ x 40.
Whitney Museum of American Art.

CHARLES BURCHFIELD: *Old House by Creek*.
1932-38. Oil. 34½ x 57.
Whitney Museum of American Art.

BEN SHAHN: *The Passion of Sacco and Vanzetti.*
1931-1932. Tempera. 84½ x 48.
Whitney Museum of American Art.

GEORGE GROSZ: *Peace, II.*
1946. Oil. 47 x 33¼.
Whitney Museum of American Art.

PHILIP EVERGOOD: *The New Lazarus.*
1927-1954. Oil. 48 x 83¼.
Whitney Museum of American Art.

5 New Forces

From the early 1920's until the late 1930's, advanced trends in American art were in the definite minority, and most painting and sculpture were representational. Representational art, however, included a wide variety of personalities, viewpoints and styles. Academicians still clung to nineteenth-century naturalistic concepts. But there were many other representational artists who were far from academic. These creative representationalists shared in the formal discoveries of the time; they knew that art was not the imitation of nature, that form and design were fundamental, and that representation without them was valueless. But they believed that there need be no conflict beween representation and formal elements. They were aware that the great art of the past had never been mere naturalism, that even in its most realistic tradition, that of Europe since the early Renaissance, realism had been united with design — three-dimensional design, in round form and deep space as well as in color, line and pattern — all physical elements which speak directly to the senses. Such design, they believed, could be achieved within a representational style, as it had been through the centuries.

These beliefs were articulated clearly by certain leading teachers. Kenneth Hayes Miller devoted a lifetime to the study and teaching of principles of form and design, particularly as exemplified in the Renaissance masters; and in his own painting applied these principles to contemporary city subjects. John Sloan when nearing sixty completely transformed his art, turning from urban genre to concentration on the figure and its plastic qualities; and in his teaching instilled these ideas into many of the rising generation. Reginald Marsh, also an active teacher, painted the crowded multitudinous life of New York in a style whose rich profusion of forms and continuous movement showed his devotion to Rubens and the baroque. Among the regionalists, Thomas H. Benton consciously incorporated his Mid-West subject-matter in forms related to the High Renaissance. Edward Hopper, while never a teacher, combined unsparing realism with deeply pondered design, powerful in its stark rectilinear and angular character — traits which were not softened with the years but grew more clearly geometric and more complex. With these painters and many others, representation continued to be a vital element in American art.

Although the social school of the 1930's was no longer a dominant movement by the end of the decade, it continued to have its vigorous individuals, as it still does today. Since the political and social upheavals of the 1930's and 1940's, social content has remained an important factor in much contemporary American art. It is no longer the simple affirmation or protest of thirty years ago; the viewpoints are more personal and diverse, marked by more drastic realism on the one hand and more imaginative fantasy on the other. There has been a pervading sense of the human situation in our time: the tensions and anxieties of today's world, the horror of the two greatest wars in history, the fears for the survival of civilization. These vast issues have been reflected in much contemporary art, though often in disguised or ambiguous forms. They have been expressed directly and powerfully in George Grosz's horror-laden memories of the first World War and his prophetic visions of the second; and in Jack Levine's biting satires on the ruling forces of society, which combine acute realism with rich sensuousness of color and pigment.

Social content has been given expression in less direct, more symbolic forms in the work of other artists: Ben Shahn's imaginative parables of the contemporary world, in which an enlightened awareness of the dilemma of modern man is based on a deeply Biblical moral sense; Philip Evergood's embodiment of passionate convictions in fantastic imagery; and Peter Blume's rich and elaborate allegories. Such artists reveal imagination, irony and philosophic content quite different from the social protest of the 1930's. The change is evident in comparing the generous bitter indignation and powerful simplicity of Shahn's *The Passion of Sacco and Vanzetti*, one of the great monuments of the social school, with his later complex symbolism.

Parallel with the modern movement's revolution in artistic language had occurred a revolution in imagery. Just as there was a liberation from naturalism in form and design, there was also a liberation from the naturalistic representation of actualities. The objective facts of the external world were transformed by the subjective fantasies of the inner world of the mind. We all know the inexhaustible profusion of visual images that rise to consciousness in dreams and half-waking states — a creative activity of the subconscious mind, without conscious volition. Such imagery, embodying our deepest desires and conflicts, has an affinity to art; as Nietzsche said, in his dreams every man is an artist. This world of imagery, drawn on by much great art of the past, had been lost in the literal naturalism of the nineteenth century, and its rediscovery was one of the fundamental contributions of our century.

In Europe the process had begun almost simultaneously with modernism. It was allied with modern psychology, particularly the exploration of the subconscious through psychoanalysis. Then in 1916 came Dada, product of the disillusion and despair of war and postwar years. Aimed at the annihilation of all accepted values, it was primarily destructive; but in this it carried seeds for the future. Its anti-rationalism prepared the way for surrealism, a systematic movement using subconscious imagery as material for art.

One root of Dada had originated in 1915 in New York, where Marcel Duchamp and Francis Picabia lived during the war, and where they and the American Man Ray launched a proto-Dada movement. After the war all three played active parts in the movement abroad. Dada, however, remained an exotic in the United States, which had not been shaken by the war as much as Europe, and which did not have the burden of a great historic past to revolt against. But the New York group's ideas, and their actual works such as Duchamp's "ready-mades," Picabia's irrational machine images and Man Ray's aerographs, were prophetic of later developments, particularly Pop art.

Surrealism, launched in Paris in 1924, did not become acclimated here until several of its European leaders arrived in the late 1930's and early 1940's: Yves Tanguy, Eugene Berman and Kurt Seligmann to remain here; Salvador Dali, André Masson and Max Ernst to stay for varying periods. But long before that, independent native manifestations of the trend toward free imagery had appeared. These Americans were not connected with the organized movements of Dada and surrealism; they were individuals, unconnected even with one another. They had neither Dada's destructive motivations nor surrealism's link with psychoanalysis; they were expressing the general spirit of the time. There was Louis M. Eilshemius with his naive fantasies, at first idyllic, then after continual rejection by the official art world, more and more tragic and violent — nightmares of jealousy, murder and death. There was Ivan Le Lorraine Albright, who by the middle 1920's was creating his compelling images of age and decay, with their elaboration of macabre realistic detail executed with extraordinary technical skill and perfection of artistry. There was Edwin Dickinson, a traditionalist whose subject-matter was far removed from academic conventions: a visionary world of ambiguous figures and objects, painted with a command of form and design recalling the masters of baroque. And there was Peter Blume, closer to surrealism than any other American-trained painter, but never part of

the movement. Blume's whole approach was conscious and rational; his allegories were logically conceived, complex in imagery, and executed with the precision and detail of the fifteenth-century Italian and Flemish masters.

The freeing of imagery in our time has had a wide effect on artists who were not surrealists. It has restored fantasy to the role it occupied in much great art of the past; it has opened up the storehouse of myth and legend, and the collective imagination of mankind; it has replaced the wornout symbols of neo-classicism with living symbols, related to the inner reality of the human mind. American art of the past quarter-century has shown an inventiveness of ideas and imagery that was lacking in the literal naturalism of the early years of the century.

The first abstract movement in the United States had lasted only about a decade, and from about 1920 until the early 1930's little abstract art was produced in this country. The dominant schools — regionalism, the American scene, the social school — were not only representational but concerned with native subject-matter. But abstract art, like music, is an international language, with little reference to specific content or place. Cultural nationalism and insistence on social content were equally hostile to abstraction, and its few adherents were like members of an underground movement.

Of its pioneers, Dove in this country and Patrick Henry Bruce in Paris remained faithful. But about 1930 a few of their fellow modernists turned toward abstraction. Alfred Maurer, who had been an early fauve in Paris, experimented with geometric patterns. Another fauve, Arthur B. Carles, who had evolved a decorative art of still-life and flowers, transformed the same motifs into luxuriant fauvist abstractions.

Of a younger generation, Stuart Davis developed his individual brand of abstraction without any early foreign experience. As a student of Henri he had found in the Armory Show "the greatest single influence I have experienced in my work." But Davis was always his own man — inventive, positive, humorous, with a grasp of the tangible realities of the contemporary United States. His innate plastic sense matured by independent thinking and experiment. In the late 1920's, concentrating for a year on a single still-life of everyday objects, he developed pure geometric abstraction that foretold his future direction — design founded on actualities.

There were few other exponents of abstract art until the

early 1930's. But then the tide began to turn. Nationalism was broadening into internationalism. In Europe, abstraction had never gone into eclipse. More than a generation had passed since it began, and it was now widely practised and diversified, with its creeds formulated. Its historical inevitability as an original creation of the twentieth century had been accepted. And it was reaching the United States in ever-increasing volume, by way of exhibitions and publications. A younger generation was ready for it.

All this was reinforced by the arrival of several prominent Europeans, mostly from Germany, where the Nazis were suppressing all modern art. Even before that, in 1931, Hans Hofmann, who for years had conducted a school in Munich, came to America and soon had new schools in New York and Provincetown, becoming one of the country's most influential teachers. The Bauhaus at Dessau had been the greatest European center for the teaching of advanced art and design. Its principles were rational and functional, emphasizing clarity, precision and the geometric style. After it was closed by the Nazis in 1933 many of its leading figures found their way to the United States. Josef Albers came that year, to teach, and to develop his purely non-objective painting with its concentration on color relationships and elemental rectangular forms. Lyonel Feininger returned in 1937. László Moholy-Nagy had been a moving spirit of the Bauhaus — painter, constructivist, designer, theorist, and originator of radical new teaching methods. Arriving in 1937, he established another Bauhaus in Chicago, and in his own work demonstrated his lucid concepts of design and his imaginative use of materials. Fritz Glarner and Piet Mondrian, not of the Bauhaus but of the related tradition of De Stijl, came in 1936 and 1939 respectively; and the constructivist sculptor Naum Gabo in 1947.

By 1936 the resurgence of abstraction was strong enough to lead to the founding of the American Abstract Artists, with forty members. Almost all were pure abstractionists, rejecting representation or any imagery, and aiming at art which should exist in purely plastic terms — by the physical materials of which it was composed, their properties of shape, color and texture, and the designs created out of these elements. These artists' belief in the creed of abstraction had an almost religious fervor — and their corresponding scorn of representational art. In opposition to the social school they saw no necessity for social content, or indeed for any specific relation to society. This attitude can be seen partly as a reaction to the disturbed state of the world; in pure plastic creation they were producing aesthetic order independent of outer chaos — one of the artist's immemorial functions.

Curiously enough in view of later developments, many of them were working in geometric styles, consciously planned, precise, sharp-edged, rectilinear or with geometric curves. The painters concentrated on the flat surface of the picture, avoiding sensations of deep space or round form, and at the most creating patterns of superimposed flat planes. A number were constructivists, using physical three-dimensional materials.

This prevalence of geometric style in the 1930's can be ascribed to several factors. The style was logical, clear, direct. It was pure, without suggestions of imagery. And it was related to the modern world, and specifically to the machine age. The nationalist and social schools had not been concerned with the aesthetics of the machine, as were the precisionists, the constructivists and the Bauhaus. But geometric abstraction, like functional architecture, was in harmony with the precision and impersonality of the machine. Except for its abstract language, it bore much the same relation to the modern United States that precisionism had. The influences of the Bauhaus, constructivism and De Stijl were unquestionable, but none of these entirely accounts for the prevalence of American geometric abstraction at this time. It was evidently the expression of one side of the American mind, as expressionism was of a quite different side. In these years it seemed that a characteristically American form of abstraction was in the making.

But simultaneously an opposite abstract tendency was making its appearance — free-form abstraction. Its origin could be traced back to early Kandinsky and the *Blaue Reiter* group, with their expression of subjective emotion, their emphasis on color, and their freedom and variety of forms. Another source was the protean genius of Picasso and his synthesis of imagery and abstract language. Surrealism also was making its contribution: an element of fantastic imagery, often transformed beyond recognition, was assimilated into free-form abstraction, enriching it not only in associative values but on the level of pure form.

A leading American pioneer of this tendency was Arshile Gorky. An ardent student of the masters, past and present, Gorky passed through successive modern influences from Cézanne to Miro; but with his sensual passion for form and color, external influences were transformed into plastic creation. His abstract works, beginning in the late 1920's, culminated in the 1940's in a personal form of surrealist abstraction in which forms from nature and images from memory and the subconscious were translated into semi-abstract design. His mature paintings such as *The Liver is the Cock's Comb* displayed prodigal inventiveness in forms, sumptuous color, and a strong graphic gift. Their freedom of forms was prophetic of the advanced tendencies of the late 1940's and the 1950's. For it was the path of free-form rather than formal abstraction that the large majority of avant-garde painters and sculptors were to take in the next decade. Just as representational expressionism had been the main road for the first generation of modernists, expressionist abstraction was to be for the second generation.

By the middle 1940's the second wave of abstract art in America was rising. The word abstraction, like expressionism, was to cover a multitude of concepts and styles, and many degrees of relationship or non-relationship to nature. As compared to the pioneer abstractionists of the 1910's, the new movement was more independent of European sources, and more radical and experimental. There had been ample time for the principles of abstraction to become acclimated, and for a new generation to attain maturity within the abstract idiom. American abstraction was to evolve individual viewpoints and styles of wide range and diversity.

Certain general characteristics were true of the movement as a whole. It was related to earlier expressionism in its emphasis on emotion, its freedom and fluidity of style, and the leading role it gave to color and pigment. But its language was purely or almost purely abstract, with little or no recognizable imagery. It concentrated on the direct visual and tactile sensations given by physical materials and by color, line and texture.

Traditional concepts of design as centralized composition of three-dimensional forms endowed with properties of solidity and weight, were abandoned. Design became open, aiming at space and movement more than substance and depth. Forms no longer rested on foundations, but existed in pictorial space. This floating character of forms appeared also in suspended or balanced sculpture such as that of Calder, Gabo and Lippold. Sometimes forms were simplified to a few elements, often of extreme power. But sometimes there were no central elements, only the overall surface activated by color and line. Mark Tobey's mystical compositions were space filled with a vibrating linear network; Mark Rothko's were space pervaded by colored light, a luminous emanation from the canvas. These innovations — emphasis on space and movement, floating forms and open design — embodied concepts of matter and energy new in our age.

With many painters, planned designing gave way to more instinctive methods, in which the physical materials and the act of manipulating them had much to do with determining the final forms — a process akin to automatic writing. (From this concept of creation as action originated the term "action painting.") Conventional use of the brush was superseded by revolutionary techniques, such as Jackson Pollock's method of pouring the pigment with wide-swinging rhythmic arm-strokes. Or again, the canvas was stained with thinned translucent pigment, achieving the luminosity and brilliance of watercolor. These inventive techniques gave new kinds of physical vitality to the painted surface. From one aspect they could be looked upon as the revolt against naturalism pushed to an extreme; from another, as a search for new means of expression inherent in the work of art as an object. These artists were conducting a more fundamental exploration into the physical elements of art than the pioneer modernists of the 1910's and 1920's. The latter had been to some extent restrained by the representational tradition of older American art, and less radical in their departures from it. But the new avant-garde was striving to build their art from the ground up, from its basis in the senses. In a way they could be considered as a fresh native manifestation of primitivism. With all their occasional over-simplifications, vacancies and brutalities, they were standing on their own feet more than any previous advanced school in America.

In many ways they were expressing certain things characteristic of the modern world and of the United States: concentration on physical sensation, love of action, speed and energy. There were analogies to jazz in the free rein given to improvization, in the emphasis on rhythm, in the repeated patterns, and in the open-ended type of composition, which one sometimes felt could go on and on, or be cut off at any point. Their sense of space seemed to reflect the spaciousness of America. It would be far-fetched to seek specific resemblances in subject or style between Thomas Cole and Jackson Pollock; but the expansive spirit that motivated our pioneer landscapists of a hundred or more years ago seemed to have been reborn in our time. Even the big scale of some of their paintings — so romantically incompatible with normal living conditions — suggested the bigness of the continent.

Parallel developments were taking place in sculpture. For centuries sculpture (at least in the European tradition) had been conceived of as the more or less naturalistic representation of real objects, especially the human figure, in the time-honored materials of stone, bronze and wood, stressing the monumental forms of the central mass. In the United States, as we have seen, there had been little experimental sculpture, and even the liberals of the first modern movement had not departed basically from the traditional physical nature of sculpture.

In the last quarter-century, sculpture in America has undergone changes even more thorough-going than those in painting. Not only has there been a general trend to abstraction, but the fundamental concepts of sculptural form have been revolutionized. Monumentality has been replaced by fluidity. The central mass has been broken up, pierced with openings, extended. Color, long absent from neo-classic sculpture, has been re-introduced. An art that was formerly completely static has taken on movement. And light has been given a role it never had before.

New materials have been adopted that call for radically new technical methods. Metals not used in the past to any extent — iron, steel, brass, copper — have been shaped and welded with the torch by sculptors such as Herbert Ferber, David Hare, Ibram Lassaw, Seymour Lipton and Theodore Roszak. Their inventive use of these previously unexploited metals and methods has produced some of the most original sculpture of our time, with a freedom of forms and an imaginative use of semi-abstract imagery parallel to free-form abstract painting.

By other sculptors everyday materials such as plastics, glass and cement have been employed in building their constructions. Natural objects like stones and tree-roots have been made the starting-points for creation. Machine-made products — automobile fenders, plumbing supplies, boiler sections, cogwheels — have been transformed into fantastic assemblages. It would be hard to name any type of *objet trouvé*, whether natural or man-made, that has not been incorporated into sculpture. At the opposite extreme, constructivists like Naum Gabo and Richard Lippold have designed precise elaborate structures in metal and plastic wire, relying on tensions and balances as in bridge-building.

In 1931 Alexander Calder, son and grandson of American sculptors, built in Paris his first moving constructions, christened "mobiles" by Marcel Duchamp. Suspended metal structures whose inventive gay and witty shapes move in the wind like the leaves of a tree, Calder's mobiles constituted a major break-through in sculptural form. A work of sculp-

ture was no longer necessarily a solid static object resting on a pedestal. Since then, moving and floating forms have become features of much contemporary sculpture. Mechanized motion has been employed by artists such as José de Rivera and Len Lye, whose revolving pieces present fascinating changing shapes. That such kinetic sculpture is only in its infancy is indicated by many recent ingenious applications of motion.

Light plays a new role. Gabo's and Lippold's intricate wire constructions were designed to catch light and thus to become creations primarily in light instead of solid forms. When Lippold also added motion in his *Moon* and *Sun*, his art became as purely one of light and movement as the motion picture. Recently the function of light has been extended beyond the subordinate role of illuminating constructions to the use of actual light in tubes and bulbs to create designs of changing colored lights.

These are by no means all the myriad innovations in materials, methods and basic concepts developed by American sculptors in the last two decades, and with constantly increasing tempo at the present time. Some of them unquestionably verge on the field of engineering and even gadgetry, and their use for artistic purposes is still problematical. But these innovations have so enormously broadened the horizons of sculpture that one cannot yet see any limits to the technical resources it can command. Never has American sculpture shown such vitality and inventiveness as today, or such promise for the future.

The advanced abstract school in painting and sculpture is international, but some of its strongest exponents have been American. It was the first international movement in which the artists of the United States not only participated on their home grounds, but were in the vanguard. In these new art forms, in which traditional values are minimal and personal creativity is the main criterion, American artists have been more on an equality with their European counterparts than in the past. With the exception of the few surviving pioneers of European modernism such as Picasso, American artists today do not look upon the current leaders abroad with the reverence that their predecessors had for the fauves and cubists. On the other hand, the new American school of painting and sculpture was the first to receive substantial recognition in Europe, through exhibitions and sales — a fundamental reversal of the international balance of art.

With the decade of the 1960's other innovating tendencies

have begun to make themselves felt. In reaction against the instinctivism and relative amorphism of free-form abstract painting there has been a return to the logic and definiteness of precise geometric abstraction, but now on a much bigger scale and with greater physical impact in brilliant color and large simplified forms — qualities partly inherited from free-form abstraction. A simultaneous development in sculpture is what has been called primary structure: basic highly simplified forms in metal or synthetic materials, sometimes machine-fabricated, purely rectilinear and angular, and often combined with strong color. In both these developments, planned architectonic design, objective and impersonal, has replaced the extreme subjectivity of free-form abstraction. Whether this will be the major future direction of abstract art, or simply another swing of the pendulum, only time can tell.

Parallel with these tendencies toward formal structure has been the phenomenal development of optical art, commonly known as Op. The scientific principles on which it is based are not new discoveries; in painting they go back to the impressionists and neo-impressionists, if not earlier. What is new is their application to abstract art. Concentration on optical sensations is a logical outgrowth of pure abstraction; one can see this exemplified in the evolution of one of its masters, Josef Albers. Optical art is of necessity entirely abstract and without imagery; and its essential nature tends to strictly limit the variety of its forms. Within these limits it has produced extraordinary visual achievements. It has greatly enlarged the range of purely visual sensations available to contemporary creation, and among other things brought about a renaissance in the field of color. Many artists who cannot be called primarily optical have profited by its explorations.

These recent developments in structure and optics have been within the abstract field. Though reactions from free-form abstraction, they are even more completely pure. But there have been other innovating movements which are opposed to the basic principles of abstraction. The most active is Pop Art, which has also been called the New American Realism. In many respects it is the complete opposite of abstraction. Where the latter in its search for purely artistic values disregarded the actualities of the external world and of contemporary America, Pop Art uses the most common banal features of our daily life in the United States — advertisements, comic strips, billboards, canned goods, soft drinks, automobiles, kitchenware, bathroom fixtures — to produce

an art that, in one aspect, is a devastating commentary on American life, both bitter and funny. Like the regionalists and the American scene school of the 1920's and 1930's, the attitude of these artists toward their native environment is ambivalent — a mixture of derision and fascination. The overwhelming omnipresence of mass-produced things and slogans and ideas and all the gadgetry that is the fine flower of a prosperous materialistic society, is to them a rich jungle of raw material for their art. As their artistic language they have adopted the use of actual objects — a method originated by the Dada movement fifty years earlier, but which they have embraced completely and used with much greater range and variety, expanding it into elaborate large-scale constructions in three dimensions, entire environments in real or simulated objects. This has been a revolution in the physical nature of the work of art that may foretell far-reaching future results. Like any innovating school, Pop Art has its element of shock-for-shock's-sake; but in the hands of its most gifted exponents it is producing an art which is at once a revealing exposé of our mass culture, and the creation from it of a new kind of artistic order. In its own way it is the most indigenous recent artistic expression of one aspect of the United States, and as such has received wide if mixed reception in other countries.

Pop art, Op art, abstraction, expressionism, representational art, and all their variations — one of the characteristics of the American art scene today is its wide diversity. The swift successive movements of the twentieth century have resulted in the phenomenon of an advance guard, a rear guard and a middle guard all existing simultaneously, if not always peaceably. Some of the leading figures have remained relatively little affected by current trends. Contemporary art in the United States includes individuals and whole schools of many different viewpoints, all having their measure of creativity and validity. This pluralistic art is the product of a democratic society, which in spite of all its pressures for uniformity, remains free and fluid, giving wide scope to individualism.

EDWIN DICKINSON: *The Fossil Hunters.*
1926-28. Oil. 96½ x 73¾.
Whitney Museum of American Art.

ANDREW WYETH: *Winter Fields.*
1942. Tempera. 17¼ x 41.
Collection of Benno C. Schmidt.

RAPHAEL SOYER: *Farewell to Lincoln Square.*
1959. Oil. 60 x 55.
The Joseph H. Hirshhorn Foundation.

JACK LEVINE: *Witches' Sabbath*.
1963. Oil. 96 x 84.
Collection of The Honorable and Mrs. William Benton.

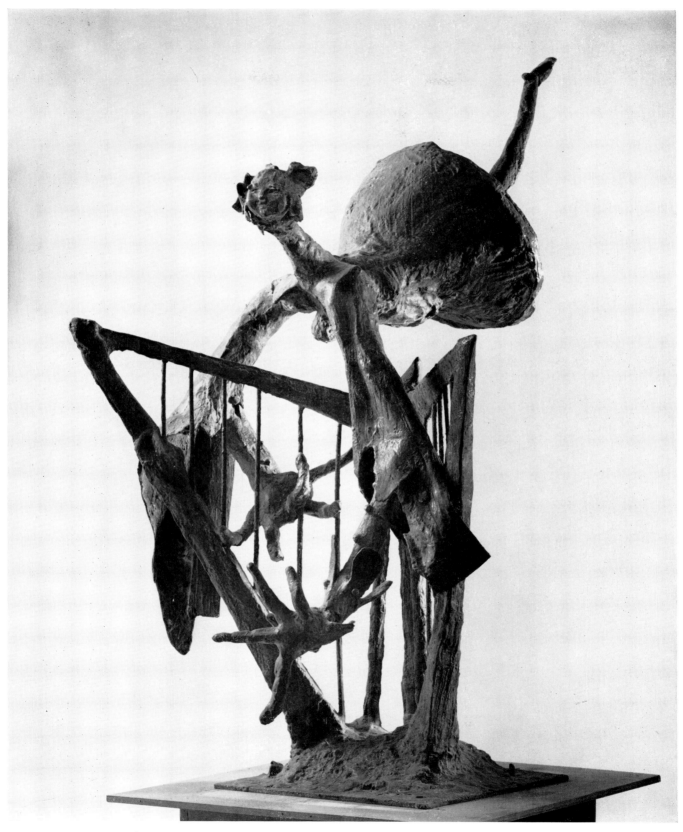

BERNARD REDER: *Harp Player, II.*
1960. Bronze. 84 high.
Whitney Museum of American Art.

YASUO KUNIYOSHI: *Amazing Juggler.*
1952. Oil. 65 x 40¼.
Des Moines Art Center.

LOREN MAC IVER: *Venice.*
1949. Oil. 59 x 93.
Whitney Museum of American Art.

JACQUES LIPCHITZ: *Sacrifice, II.*
1948/52. Bronze. 49¼ high.
Whitney Museum of American Art.

ABRAHAM RATTNER: *Song of Esther.*
1958. Oil. 60 x 48.
Whitney Museum of American Art.

IVAN ALBRIGHT: *Poor Room — There is No Time, No End, No Today,*
No Yesterday, Only the Forever, and Forever and Forever without End.
1941-43, 1948-55, 1957-62. Oil. 48 x 37.
Collection of Mr. and Mrs. Ivan Albright.

YVES TANGUY: *Fear.*
1949. Oil. 60 x 40.
Whitney Museum of American Art.

PETER BLUME: *Passage to Etna.*
1956. Oil. 78 x 38⅝.
Fogg Art Museum.

STUART DAVIS: *Ouh! in San Pao.*
1951. Oil. 52¼ x 41¾.
Whitney Museum of American Art.

ALEXANDER CALDER: *The Cock's Comb.*
1960. Sheet iron. 146½ long.
Whitney Museum of American Art.

LEE GATCH: *Greenhouse.*
1950. Oil. 44 x 36.
Collection of Mr. and Mrs. Roy R. Neuberger.

MORRIS GRAVES: *Flight of Plover.*
1955. Oil. 36 x 48.
Whitney Museum of American Art.

MARK TOBEY: *Universal Field.*
949. Tempera, pastel. 28 x 44.
Whitney Museum of American Art.

JACKSON POLLOCK: *Blue Poles*.
1953. Oil, duco, glass. 84 x 192.
Collection of Mr. and Mrs. Ben Heller.

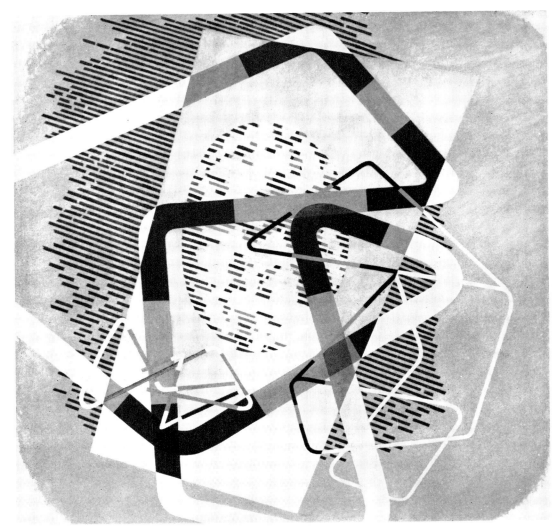

LASZLO MOHOLY-NAGY: *Space Modulator.*
1938-40. Oil. 47 x 47.
Whitney Museum of American Art.

ISAMU NOGUCHI: *Humpty Dumpty.*
1946. Slate. 58¾ high.
Whitney Museum of American Art.

NAUM GABO: *Linear Construction in Space, Number 4.*
1958. Plastic, stainless steel. 40 high.
Whitney Museum of American Art.

ARSHILE GORKY: *The Liver is the Cock's Comb.*
1944. Oil. 72 x 98.
Albright-Knox Art Gallery.

ROBERT MOTHERWELL: *The Voyage.*
1949. Oil, tempera. 48 x 94.
The Museum of Modern Art.

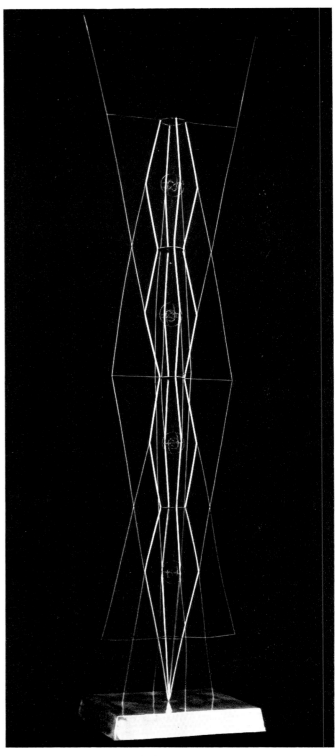

THEODORE ROSZAK: *Sea Sentinel*.
1956. Steel, bronze. 105 high.
Whitney Museum of American Art.

RICHARD LIPPOLD: *Primordial Figure*.
1947-48. Brass, copper wire. 96 high.
Whitney Museum of American Art.

RAOUL HAGUE: *Sawkill Walnut.*
1955. Walnut. 42 high.
Whitney Museum of American Art.

MICHAEL LEKAKIS: *Sympan.*
1960. Oak. 86 high.
Whitney Museum of American Art.

CLYFFORD STILL: *Number 2.*
1949. Oil. 96 x 69.
Collection of Mr. and Mrs. Ben Heller.

WILLEM DE KOONING: *Door to the River.*
1960. Oil. 80 x 70.
Whitney Museum of American Art.

REUBEN NAKIAN: *Olympia.*
1960-62. Bronze. 72 high.
Whitney Museum of American Art.

DAVID SMITH: *Lectern Sentinel.*
1961. Stainless steel. 101¾ high.
Whitney Museum of American Art.

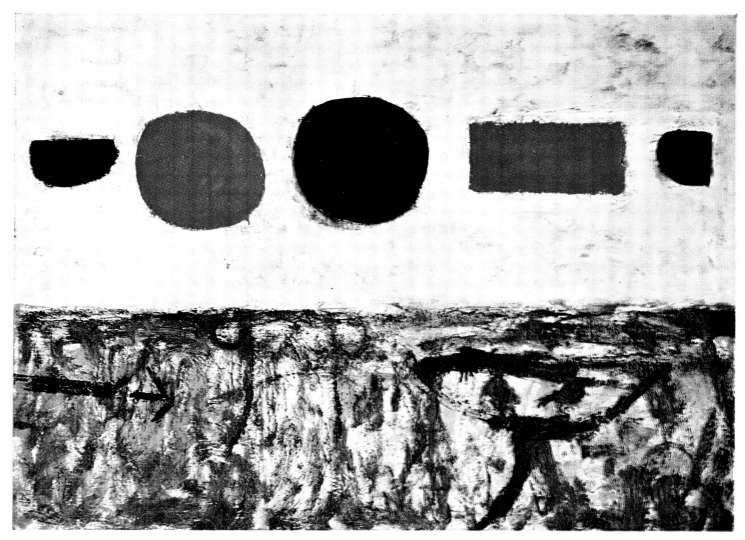

ADOLPH GOTTLIEB: *The Frozen Sounds, Number 1.*
1951. Oil. 36 x 48.
Whitney Museum of American Art.

FRANZ KLINE: *Dahlia.*
1959. Oil. 82 x 67.
Whitney Museum of American Art.

HERBERT FERBER: *Homage to Piranesi, III.*
1963. Copper. 104 high.
Collection of Herbert Ferber.

SEYMOUR LIPTON: *Gateway.*
1964. Bronze. 76 high.
Marlborough-Gerson Gallery.

JASPER JOHNS: *Studio*.
1964. Oil. 73½ x 145½.
Whitney Museum of American Art.

GEORGE SEGAL: *Girl in Doorway.*
1965. Plaster, wood, glass, aluminum paint. 113 high.
Whitney Museum of American Art.

MARISOL: *Women and Dog.*
1964. Wood, plaster, synthetic polymer paint, miscellaneous items. 91 long.
Whitney Museum of American Art.

LARRY RIVERS: *Africa II.*
1962-63. Oil. 112¾ x 153.
Marlborough-Gerson Gallery.

ROBERT RAUSCHENBERG: *Tracer*.
1963. Oil. 84 x 60.
Collection of Mr. and Mrs. Frank M. Titelman.

JIM DINE: *Double Isometric Self Portrait (Serape)*
1964. Oil, wood, metal. 57 x 84.
Collection of Mrs. Robert M. Benjamin.

ROBERT INDIANA: *The X-5.*
1963. Oil. 108 x 108.
Whitney Museum of American Art.

LOUISE NEVELSON: *Young Shadows.*
1959-60. Wood. 115 x 126.
Whitney Museum of American Art.

AL HELD: *The Dowager Empress.*
1965. Synthetic polymer paint. 96 x 72.
Whitney Museum of American Art.

JAMES WINES: *Sabre I.*
1965-66. Iron, cement. 110 long.
Marlborough-Gerson Gallery.

ROBERT MORRIS: *Untitled.*
1966. Reinforced Fiberglas, polyester resin. 36 x 48 x 90.
Whitney Museum of American Art.

Index of the Illustrations

Paintings are in oil unless otherwise specified. Dimensions are in inches, height preceding width. The largest dimension of sculpture is given.

PAINTINGS

IVAN ALBRIGHT. Born 1897.

Poor Room — There is No Time, No End, No Today, No Yesterday, Only the Forever, and Forever and Forever without End. 1941-43, 1948-55, 1957-62. 48 x 37.

Collection of Mr. and Mrs. Ivan Albright.　　114

WASHINGTON ALLSTON. 1799-1843.

Elijah in the Desert. 1818. 48¾ x 72½.

Museum of Fine Arts, Boston.　　21

ANONYMOUS.

John Van Cortlandt. c. 1731. 57 x 40¹⁵⁄₁₆.

The Brooklyn Museum, New York.　　14

ANONYMOUS.

Mrs. Elizabeth Paddy Wensley. 1670-80. 42¼ x 33¾

Pilgrim Society, Plymouth, Mass.　　13

THOMAS HART BENTON. Born 1889.

Preparing the Bill. 1934. 46 x 38.

Randolph-Macon Woman's College, Lynchburg, Va.　　95

ALBERT BIERSTADT. 1830-1902.

The Buffalo Trail — The Impending Storm. 1869. 29½ x 49½.

The Corcoran Gallery of Art, Washington, D.C., gift of Mr. and Mrs. Lansdell K. Christie.　　33

GEORGE CALEB BINGHAM. 1811-1879.

Raftsmen Playing Cards. 1847. 28 x 36.

City Art Museum of St. Louis, Ezra H. Linley Fund.　　34

RALPH A. BLAKELOCK. 1847-1919.

Ecstasy. 30 x 38.

The Hackley Art Gallery, Muskegon, Mich.　　54

PETER BLUME. Born 1906.

Passage to Etna. 1956. 78 x 38⅝.

Fogg Art Museum, Harvard University.　　115

DAVID G. BLYTHE. 1815-1865.
The Pittsburgh Horse Market. c. 1858. 26½ x 36½.
Collection of Thomas M. Evans. 34

CHARLES BURCHFIELD. Born 1893.
Old House by Creek. 1932-38. 34½ x 57.
Whitney Museum of American Art. 97

MARY CASSATT. 1845-1926.
The Bath. c. 1891-92. 39½ x 26.
The Art Institute of Chicago, Robert A. Waller Fund. 64

Young Women Picking Fruit. 1891. 51¼ x 35¾.
Museum of Art, Carnegie Institute, Pittsburgh. 63

WILLIAM M. CHASE. 1849-1916.
Hide and Seek. 1888. 27½ x 36.
The Phillips Collection, Washington, D.C. 67

FREDERIC E. CHURCH. 1826-1900.
Rainy Season in the Tropics. 1866. 55 x 84.
Collection of Mr. and Mrs. J. William Middendorf II. 36

THOMAS COLE. 1801-1848.
The Oxbow (The Connecticut River near Northampton).
1836. 51½ x 76.
The Metropolitan Museum of Art, gift of Mrs. Russell
Sage, 1909. 30

JOHN SINGLETON COPLEY. 1738-1815.
Mrs. Ezekiel Goldthwait. 1770-71. 50 x 39¾.
Museum of Fine Arts, Boston. 18

Mr. and Mrs. Thomas Mifflin. 1773. 60½ x 48.
Historical Society of Pennsylvania, Philadelphia. 17

STUART DAVIS. 1894-1964.
Owh! in San Paõ. 1951. 52¼ x 41¾.
Whitney Museum of American Art. 116

WILLEM DE KOONING. Born 1904.
Door to the River. 1960. 80 x 70.
Whitney Museum of American Art, gift of the Friends of
the Whitney Museum of American Art (and purchase). 129

CHARLES DEMUTH. 1883-1935.
My Egypt. 1927. 35¾ x 30.
Whitney Museum of American Art. 93

THOMAS W. DEWING. 1885-1938.
The Recitation. 1891. 30 x 55.
The Detroit Institute of Arts. 67

EDWIN DICKINSON. Born 1891.
The Fossil Hunters. 1926-28. 96½ x 73¾.
Whitney Museum of American Art. 106

JIM DINE. Born 1935.
Double Isometric Self Portrait (Serape). 1964.
Oil, wood, metal. 57 x 84.
Collection of Mrs. Robert M. Benjamin. 142

ASHER B. DURAND. 1796-1886.
Kindred Spirits. 1849. 46 x 36.
The New York Public Library, Astor, Lenox and Tilden
Foundations. 32

JOHN DURAND. Active 1766-1782.
The Rapalje Children. c. 1768. 50¾ x 40.
The New-York Historical Society, New York. 16

FRANK DUVENECK. 1848-1919.
Amy Folsom. c. 1880. 36 x 23¾.
The Montclair Art Museum, Montclair, N. J. 59

THOMAS EAKINS. 1844-1916.
Miss Van Buren. c. 1889-91. 45 x 32.
The Phillips Collection, Washington, D.C. 65

The Swimming Hole. 1883. 27 x 36.
Fort Worth Art Association, Fort Worth, Texas. 66

RALPH EARL. 1751-1801.
*Chief Justice Oliver Ellsworth and his Wife, Abigail Wol-
cott.* 1792. 75¹⁵⁄₁₆ x 86¾.
Wadsworth Atheneum, Hartford, Conn. 22

EDWIN ROMANZO ELMER. 1850-1923.
Mourning Picture. c. 1889. 28 x 36.
Smith College Museum of Art, Northampton, Mass. 37

PHILIP EVERGOOD. Born 1901.

The New Lazarus. 1927-54. 48 x 83¼.

Whitney Museum of American Art, gift of Joseph H.
Hirshhorn.   99

ROBERT FEKE. Active 1741-1750.

Isaac Royall and His Family. 1741. 56³⁄₁₆ x 77¾.

Harvard University Law School, Cambridge, Mass.   15

LEE GATCH. Born 1902.

Greenhouse. 1950. 44 x 36.

Collection of Mr. and Mrs. Roy R. Neuberger.   118

WILLIAM J. GLACKENS. 1870-1938.

Hammerstein's Roof Garden. c. 1901. 30 x 25.

Whitney Museum of American Art.   78

ARSHILE GORKY. 1904-1948.

The Liver is the Cock's Comb. 1944. 72 x 98.

Albright-Knox Art Gallery, Buffalo, N. Y.   124

ADOLPH GOTTLIEB. Born 1903.

The Frozen Sounds, Number 1. 1951. 36 x 48.

Whitney Museum of American Art, gift of Mr. and Mrs.
Samuel M. Kootz.   132

MORRIS GRAVES. Born 1910.

Flight of Plover. 1955. 36 x 48.

Whitney Museum of American Art, gift of Mr. and Mrs.
Roy R. Neuberger.   119

GEORGE GROSZ. 1893-1959.

Peace, II. 1946. 47 x 33¼.

Whitney Museum of American Art.   99

JOHN HABERLE. 1856-1933.

A Bachelor's Drawer. 1894. 20 x 36.

Collection of Mr. and Mrs. J. William Middendorf II.   41

WILLIAM M. HARNETT. 1848-1892.

After the Hunt. 1885. 71 x 48.

California Palace of the Legion of Honor, San Francisco,
Mildred Anna Williams Collection.   40

MARSDEN HARTLEY. 1877-1943.

Painting, Number 5. 1914-15. 39½ x 31¾.

Whitney Museum of American Art, anonymous gift.   84

CHILDE HASSAM. 1859-1935.

The Summer Girl. 1894. 32 x 32.

Collection of Mr. and Mrs. Ogden Phipps.   70

MARTIN J. HEADE. 1819-1904.

View of Tree Fern Walk, Jamaica. 1887. 53 x 90.

Collection of Patrick A. Doheny.   33

AL HELD. Born 1928.

The Dowager Empress. 1965. Synthetic polymer paint.
96 x 72.

Whitney Museum of American Art, gift of the Friends of
the Whitney Museum of American Art.   144

EDWARD HICKS. 1780-1849.

The Peaceable Kingdom. 1840-45. 30⅛ x 34½.

New York State Historical Association, Cooperstown,
N. Y.   37

WINSLOW HOMER. 1836-1910.

The Fox Hunt. 1893. 38 x 68.

Pennsylvania Academy of the Fine Arts, Philadelphia.   60

West Point, Prout's Neck. 1900. 30 x 48.

Sterling and Francine Clark Art Institute,
Williamstown, Mass.   61

EDWARD HOPPER. Born 1882.

Early Sunday Morning. 1930. 35 x 60.

Whitney Museum of American Art.   96

WILLIAM MORRIS HUNT. 1824-1879.

Anahita, or The Flight of Night. 1878. 62⅝ x 95¼.

Museum of Fine Arts, Boston.   51

ROBERT INDIANA. Born 1928.

The X-5. 1963. 108 x 108.

Whitney Museum of American Art.   142

GEORGE INNESS. 1825-1894.

Early Morning, Tarpon Springs. 1892. 42 x 32¼.

The Art Institute of Chicago, Edward B. Butler
Collection.   49

The Monk. 1873. 39½ x 64.

Addison Gallery of American Art, Phillips Academy,
Andover, Mass., gift of Stephen C. Clark.   49

JASPER JOHNS. Born 1930.
Studio. 1964. 73½ x 145½.
Whitney Museum of American Art, gift of the Friends of the Whitney Museum of American Art (and purchase).   136-137

EASTMAN JOHNSON.
Sugaring-off, Number 2. 1865-75. 33 x 54.
Butler Institute of American Art, Youngstown, Ohio.   55

MORRIS KANTOR. Born 1896.
Synthetic Arrangement. 1923. 46 x 54.
Collection of Mr. and Mrs. Arthur G. Altschul.   83

FRANZ KLINE. 1910-1962.
Dahlia. 1959. 82 x 67.
Whitney Museum of American Art, gift of an anonymous group of Friends of the Whitney Museum of American Art.   133

YASUO KUNIYOSHI. 1890-1953.
Amazing Juggler. 1952. 65 x 40¼.
Edmundson Collection, Des Moines Art Center, Des Moines, Iowa.   110

ERNEST LAWSON. 1873-1939.
High Bridge. 1934. 30 x 40.
Whitney Museum of American Art.   79

JACK LEVINE. Born 1915.
Witches' Sabbath. 1963. 96 x 84.
Collection of The Honorable and Mrs. William Benton. 108

GEORGE LUKS. 1867-1933.
Armistice Night. 1918. 37 x 68¾.
Whitney Museum of American Art, anonymous gift.   79

LOREN MACIVER. Born 1909.
Venice. 1949. 59 x 93.
Whitney Museum of American Art.   111

MAN RAY. Born 1890.
The Rope Dancer Accompanies Herself with Her Shadows. 1916. 52 x 73⅜.
The Museum of Modern Art, gift of G. David Thompson.   85

JOHN MARIN. 1870-1953.
Region of Brooklyn Bridge Fantasy. 1932. Watercolor. 18¾ x 22¼.
Whitney Museum of American Art.   89

REGINALD MARSH. 1898-1954.
Human Pool Tables. 1938. Egg tempera. 29¾ x 40.
Whitney Museum of American Art, gift of Mrs. Reginald Marsh and William Benton.   97

HOMER D. MARTIN. 1836-1897.
The Iron Mine, Port Henry, New York. 30 x 50.
National Collection of Fine Arts, Smithsonian Institution, Washington, D.C.   48

LASZLO MOHOLY-NAGY. 1895-1946.
Space Modulator. 1938-40. 47 x 47.
Whitney Museum of American Art, gift of Mrs. Sybil Moholy-Nagy.   122

SAMUEL F. B. MORSE. 1791-1872.
The Muse — Susan Walker Morse. c. 1835-37. 73¾ x 57⅝.
The Metropolitan Museum of Art, bequest of Herbert L. Pratt, 1945.   31

ROBERT MOTHERWELL. Born 1915.
The Voyage. 1949. Oil, tempera. 48 x 94.
The Museum of Modern Art, gift of Mrs. John D. Rockefeller, 3rd.   125

WILLIAM SIDNEY MOUNT. 1807-1868.
Eel Spearing at Setauket. 1845. 29 x 36.
New York State Historical Association, Cooperstown, N. Y.   35

GEORGIA O'KEEFFE. Born 1887.
Abstraction. 1926. 30 x 18.
Whitney Museum of American Art.   92

WILLIAM PAGE. 1811-1885.
Self Portrait. c. 1860. 59 x 36.
The Detroit Institute of Arts.   50

Mrs. William Page. c. 1860. 60¼ x 36¼.
The Detroit Institute of Arts.   50

CHARLES WILLSON PEALE. 1741-1827.
Exhuming the Mastodon. 1806. 50 x 62½.
The Peale Museum, Baltimore, gift of Mrs. Harry White.   20

RAPHAELLE PEALE. 1774-1825.
After the Bath. 1823. 29 x 24.
Nelson Gallery — Atkins Museum, Kansas City,
(Nelson Fund).   41

JACKSON POLLOCK. 1912-1956.
Blue Poles. 1953. Oil, duco, glass. 84 x 192.
Collection of Mr. and Mrs. Ben Heller.   120-121

MAURICE PRENDERGAST. 1859-1924.
The Promenade. 1913. 30 x 34.
Whitney Museum of American Art, bequest of Alexander
M. Bing.   81

ABRAHAM RATTNER. Born 1895.
Song of Esther. 1958. 60 x 48.
Whitney Museum of American Art, gift of the Friends
of the Whitney Museum of American Art.   113

ROBERT RAUSCHENBERG. Born 1925.
Tracer. 1963. 84 x 60.
Collection of Mr. and Mrs. Frank M. Titelman.   141

LARRY RIVERS. Born 1923.
Africa II. 1962-63. 112¾ x 133.
Marlborough-Gerson Gallery, New York.   140

THEODORE ROBINSON. 1852-1896.
On the Towpath — A Halt. 1893-94. 28 x 40.
Collection of Mr. and Mrs. Cornelius Vanderbilt
Whitney.   62

ALBERT P. RYDER. 1847-1917.
The Flying Dutchman. c. 1887. 13¾ x 16½.
National Collection of Fine Arts, Smithsonian Institution,
Washington, D.C.   52

The Race Track. 1890-1910. 28¼ x 35¼.
The Cleveland Museum of Art, purchase from the J. H.
Wade Fund.   53

JOHN SINGER SARGENT. 1856-1925.
Group with Parasols. Probably 1908 or 1910. 21 x 27¾.
Collection of Rita and Daniel Fraad.   69

Mme. Edouard Pailleron. 1879. 82 x 39½.
The Corcoran Gallery of Art, Washington, D.C., Gallery
Fund, and gifts of Katherine McCook Knox, John A.
Nevius and Mr. and Mrs. Lansdell K. Christie   58

MORTON L. SCHAMBERG. 1881-1918.
Machine. 1916. 30⅛ x 22¾.
Yale University Art Gallery, collection of the
Société Anonyme.   92

BEN SHAHN. Born 1898.
The Passion of Sacco and Vanzetti. 1931-32. Tempera.
84½ x 48.
Whitney Museum of American Art, gift of Edith and
Milton Lowenthal in memory of Juliana Force.   98

CHARLES SHEELER. 1883-1965.
Classic Landscape. (Ford Rouge Plant). 1931. 25 x 32¼.
Collection of Mrs. Edsel B. Ford.   94

JOHN SLOAN. 1871-1951.
Backyards, Greenwich Village. 1914. 26 x 32.
Whitney Museum of American Art.   80

RAPHAEL SOYER. Born 1899.
Farewell to Lincoln Square. 1959. 60 x 55.
The Joseph H. Hirshhorn Foundation, New York.   107

JOSEPH STELLA. 1877-1946.
Battle of Lights, Coney Island. 1913. 76 x 84.
Yale University Art Gallery, collection of the Société
Anonyme.   82

MAURICE STERNE. 1878-1957.
Dance of the Elements. 1913. 56¾ x 65½.
North Carolina Museum of Art, Raleigh, N. C.   90

CLYFFORD STILL. Born 1904.
Number 2. 1949. 96 x 69.
Collection of Mr. and Mrs. Ben Heller.   128

GILBERT STUART. 1755-1828.

Mrs. Perez Morton. c. 1802. 29⁷/₁₆ x 24⅛.

Worcester Art Museum, Worcester, Mass., gift of the grandchildren of Joseph Tuckerman, Newport, R. I., 1899.   23

YVES TANGUY. 1900-1955.

Fear. 1949. 60 x 40.

Whitney Museum of American Art.   115

MARK TOBEY. Born 1890.

Universal Field. 1949. Tempera, pastel. 28 x 44.

Whitney Museum of American Art.   119

JOHN TRUMBULL. 1756-1843.

Sortie of the British Garrison at Gibraltar. c. 1788. 20 x 30.

Cincinnati Art Museum.   20

JOHN H. TWACHTMAN. 1853-1902.

Azaleas. c. 1898. 30 x 24.

Randolph-Macon Woman's College, Lynchburg, Va.   68

MAX WEBER. 1881-1961.

Chinese Restaurant. 1915. 40 x 48.

Whitney Museum of American Art.   88

JAMES A. McNEILL WHISTLER. 1834-1903.

Lady of the Lange Lijsen. 1864. 36¼ x 24¼.

John G. Johnson Collection, Philadelphia Museum of Art.   57

Wapping on Thames. 1861. 28 x 40.

Collection of Mr. and Mrs. John Hay Whitney.   56

GRANT WOOD. 1892-1942.

Stone City, Iowa. 1930. 30¼ x 40.

Joslyn Art Museum, Omaha, Neb.   94

ANDREW WYETH. Born 1917.

Winter Fields. 1942. Tempera. 17¼ x 41.

Collection of Benno C. Schmidt.   107

SCULPTURE

ALEXANDER CALDER. Born 1898.

The Cock's Comb. 1960. Sheet iron. 146½ long.

Whitney Museum of American Art, gift of the Friends of the Whitney Museum of American Art.   117

HERBERT FERBER. Born 1906.

Homage to Piranesi, III. 1963. Copper. 104 high.

Owned by Herbert Ferber.   134

NAUM GABO. Born 1890.

Linear Construction in Space, Number 4. 1958. Plastic, stainless steel. 40 high.

Whitney Museum of American Art, gift of the Friends of the Whitney Museum of American Art.   123

RAOUL HAGUE. Born 1905.

Sawkill Walnut. 1955. Walnut. 42 high.

Whitney Museum of American Art, gift of the Friends of the Whitney Museum of American Art.   127

GASTON LACHAISE. 1882-1935.

Standing Woman. 1912-27. Bronze. 70¼ high.

Whitney Museum of American Art.   86

MICHAEL LEKAKIS. Born 1907.

Sympan. 1960. Oak. 86 high.

Whitney Museum of American Art, gift of the Friends of the Whitney Museum of American Art.   127

JACQUES LIPCHITZ. Born 1891.

Sacrifice, II. 1948-52. Bronze. 49¼ high.

Whitney Museum of American Art.   112

RICHARD LIPPOLD. Born 1915.

Primordial Figure. 1947-48. Brass, copper wire. 96 high.

Whitney Museum of American Art, gift of the Friends of the Whitney Museum of American Art, Charles Simon (and purchase).   126

SEYMOUR LIPTON. Born 1903.
Gateway. 1964. Bronze on monel metal. 76 high.
Marlborough-Gerson Gallery, New York.   135

MARISOL. Born 1930.
Women and Dog. 1964. Wood, plaster, synthetic polymer paint, miscellaneous items. 91 long.
Whitney Museum of American Art, gift of the Friends of the Whitney Museum of American Art.   139

ROBERT MORRIS. Born 1931.
Untitled. 1966. Reinforced Fiberglas, polyester resin. 90 wide.
Whitney Museum of American Art, gift of the Howard and Jean Lipman Foundation, Inc.   145

REUBEN NAKIAN. Born 1897.
Olympia. 1960-62. Bronze. 72 high.
Whitney Museum of American Art, gift of the Friends of the Whitney Museum of American Art (and purchase).   130

LOUISE NEVELSON. Born 1900.
Young Shadows. 1959-60. Wood. 126 long.
Whitney Museum of American Art, gift of the Friends of the Whitney Museum of American Art and Charles Simon.   143

ISAMU NOGUCHI. Born 1904.
Humpty Dumpty. 1946. Ribbon slate. 58¾ high.
Whitney Museum of American Art.   123

ERASTUS DOW PALMER. 1817-1904.
The White Captive. 1859. Marble. 66 high.
The Metropolitan Museum of Art, gift of Hamilton Fish, 1894.   38

BERNARD REDER. 1897-1963.
Harp Player, II. 1960. Bronze. 84 high.
Whitney Museum of American Art.   109

WILLIAM RIMMER. 1816-1879.
The Dying Centaur. c. 1871. Bronze. 21½ high.
The Metropolitan Museum of Art, gift of Edward Holbrook, 1906.   39

HUGO ROBUS. 1885-1964.
One and Another. 1934. Bronze. 41 long.
Sara Roby Foundation, New York.   87

THEODORE ROSZAK. Born 1907.
Sea Sentinel. 1956. Steel, bronze. 105 high.
Whitney Museum of American Art.   126

WILLIAM RUSH. 1756-1833.
Comedy. 1808. Painted pine. 114 high.
The Edwin Forrest Home, courtesy of the Philadelphia Museum of Art.   19

Tragedy. 1808. Painted pine. 114 high.
The Edwin Forrest Home, courtesy of the Philadelphia Museum of Art.   19

AUGUSTUS SAINT-GAUDENS. 1847-1907.
Diana. 1892. Gilded bronze. 112 high.
The Metropolitan Museum of Art, Rogers Fund, 1927.   71

GEORGE SEGAL. Born 1924.
Girl in Doorway. 1965. Plaster, wood, glass, aluminum paint, 113 high.
Whitney Museum of American Art.   138

DAVID SMITH. 1906-1965.
Lectern Sentinel. 1961. Stainless steel. 101¾ high.
Whitney Museum of American Art, gift of the Friends of the Whitney Museum of American Art (and purchase).   131

JOHN STORRS. 1885-1956.
Composition Around Two Voids. 1932. Stainless steel. 20 high.
Whitney Museum of American Art, gift of Monique Storrs Booz.   87

JAMES WINES. Born 1932.
Sabre I. 1965-66. Iron, cement. 110 long.
Marlborough-Gerson Gallery, New York.   145

WILLIAM ZORACH. Born 1887.
The Future Generation. 1942-47. Marble. 40 high.
Whitney Museum of American Art.   91

Index of the Text

Abstraction, 45, 72, **73**, 74, 75, **101-105**
Action painting, 103
Albers, Josef, **102,** 105
Albright, Ivan Le Lorraine, 101
Allston, Washington, **12,** 43, 44
American Abstract Artists, 102
American scene, The, 28, 75, **76-77,** 101, 105
Armory Show, **73,** 74, 101
Audubon, John James, 26

Barbizon School, 25, 42, 43
Bauhaus, The, 102
Beck, George, 24
Bellows, George, 76
Benton, Thomas H., **76,** 100
Berman, Eugene, 101
Bierstadt, Albert, 25
Bingham, George Caleb, 26-27
Birch, Thomas, 24
Bishop, Isabel, 77
Blackburn, Joseph, 8
Blakelock, Ralph A., 44
Blaue Reiter. Der. 73, 74, 102
Blume, Peter, 100, 101
Blythe, David G., 27-28
Bonnard, Pierre, 72
Brancusi, Constantin, 75
Brown, Henry Kirke, 47
Brown, J. G., 28
Bruce, Patrick Henry, 73, 101
Brücke. Die, 74
Brush, George de Forest, 46
Bryant, William Cullen, 24
Burchfield, Charles, 76

Calder, Alexander, 73, 103, **104**
Canova, Antonio, 29

Carles, Arthur B., 73, **101**
Cassatt, Mary, 44, **45**
Catlin, George, 25
Cézanne, Paul, 72, 102
Chandler, Winthrop, 8
Chase, William M., 45
Church, Frederic E., 25
Classical subjects, 7, **11-12,** 29
Cole, Thomas, **24,** 43, 103
Coleman, Glenn O., 76
Constructivism, 73, 102, 104
Copley, John Singleton, 8, **9,** 11, 12, 43, 74
Corot, Camille, 25, 42
Courbet, Gustave, 27
Cubism, 72, **73, 74**
Currier, J. Frank, 45
Curry, John Steuart, 76

Dada, **101,** 105
Dali, Salvador, 101
Dasburg, Andrew, 73
Daumier, Honoré, 27, 72
David, Jacques-Louis, 9, 11, 12, 26
Davies, Arthur B., 73
Davis, Stuart, 73, **101**
Deas, Charles, 26
Degas, Hilaire Edgar, 44, 45
Delacroix, Eugène, 11, 25, 43, 44
Delaunay, Robert, 73
Demuth, Charles, 74
de Rivera, José, 104
Dewing, Thomas W., 46
Diaz de la Peña, Narcisse-Virgile, 43
Dickinson, Edwin, 101
Doughty, Thomas, 24
Dove, Arthur G., 72, **73,** 101
du Bois, Guy Pène, 76

Duchamp, Marcel, 73, 101, 104
Duchamp-Villon, Raymond, 75
Durand, Asher B., 24
Duveneck, Frank, 45

Eakins, Thomas, 10, 28, **42-43,** 44, 45, 46, 47
Earl, Ralph, **9-10,** 24
Eastman, Seth, 26
Eight, The, 72-73
Eilshemius, Louis M., 101
Ernst, Max, 101
Evergood, Philip, 77, **100**
Expressionism, 72, 73, **74-75,** 103, 105

Fantasy, **100-101,** 102
Fauves. Les. 72
Federal art projects, 76, 77
Feininger, Lyonel, 72, **73,** 102
Feke, Robert, **8,** 11, 74
Ferber, Herbert, 104
Figureheads, 10-11
Fisher, Alvin, 24
Folk art, **7-11,** 24
Fuller, George, 43
Futurism, 72, **73-74**

Gabo, Naum, 102, 103, 104
Genre, 7, **26-28,** 42, 72
Géricault, Théodore, 11, 25
Glackens, William J., 72
Glarner, Fritz, 102
Gorky, Arshile, 73, **102**
Goya y Lucientes, Francisco de, 44, 72
Greenough, Horatio, 29
Greenwood, John, 7
Groombridge, William, 24
Gropper, William, 77
Gros, Antoine Jean, 11

Grosz, George, 77, **100**
Guy, Francis, 24, 26
Gwathmey, Robert, 77

Haberle, John, 29
Hals, Frans, 45, 72
Hare, David, 104
Harnett, William M., 28-29
Hartley, Marsden, 72, **73, 75**
Hassam, Childe, 46
Haydon, Benjamin Robert, 7
Heade, Martin J., 25
Henri, Robert, **72**, 73, 74, 76, 101
Henry, E. L., 28
Historical subjects, 7, 9, **11-12**
Hofmann, Hans, 102
Homer, Winslow, **42-43**, 44, 45, 46, 47
Hopper, Edward, **76**, 77, **100**
Hudson River school, **24-25**, 42, 43, 44, 46
Hunt, William Morris, **42**, 43, 44, 45

Impressionism, 43, 44, **45-46**, 47, 72, 74
Inness, George, **42**, 43, 44, 46

Johnson, Eastman, 27, **28**

Kandinsky, Wassily, 73, 102
King, Charles Bird, 28
Kneller, Sir Godfrey, 8
Krimmel, John Lewis, 26

Lachaise, Gaston, 75
La Farge, John, 42, **44**, 45, 46, 47
Landscape, 7, 10, 12, **24-26, 42**, 43, 44, 45-46, 76, 103
Lane, Fitz Hugh, 25
Lassaw, Ibram, 104
Laurent, Robert, 75
Lawrence, Sir Thomas, 10, 45
Lawson, Ernest, 73
Leibl, Wilhelm, 45
Levine, Jack, 100
Limners, **8,** 9
Lipchitz, Jacques, 75
Lippold, Richard, 103, 104
Lipton, Seymour, 104
Luks, George, 72
Lye, Len, 104

Macdonald-Wright, Stanton, 73
Machine, The, 27, **74**, 102
Manet, Edouard, 44, 72
Man Ray, 101
Marin, John, 46, 72, **74-75**
Marsh, Reginald, 77, **100**
Martin, Homer D., **42**, 46
Masson, André, 101
Matisse, Henri, 72, 75
Maurer, Alfred, 101
Miller, Alfred J., 26
Miller, Kenneth Hayes, 100
Millet, Jean-François, 27, 42, 43, 45
Mills, Clark, 47

Miro, Joan, 102
Modernism, **72-76**, 103
Moholy-Nagy, László, 102
Mondrian, Piet, 102
Monet, Claude, 45, 46
Moran, Thomas, 25
Morse, Samuel F. B., 10, **12**, 24
Mount, William Sidney, **26**, 27
Mural painting, 11, 42, 47
Myers, Jerome, 76

Nadelman, Elie, 75
Naturalism, 42, 44
Neagle, John, 10
Neo-classicism, 11, 12, **29**
Neo-impressionism, 72
Newman, Robert Loftin, 43
Noguchi, Isamu, 73

O'Keeffe, Georgia, 73
Optical art, 105
Orozco, José Clemente, 77
Orphism, 73

Page, William, 43
Palmer, Erastus D., 29
Peale, Charles Willson, **9**, 11, 12, 28
Peale, James, 28
Peale, Raphaelle, 9, **28**
Peale, Rembrandt, 9, 12
Peale, Rubens, 28
Peale, Titian Ramsay, 28
Pelham, Peter, 9
Pennsylvania Academy of the Fine Arts, 7, 9, 43
Peto, John F., 29
Picabia, Francis, 101
Picasso, Pablo, 72, 75, 102, 104
Pollock, Jackson, 44, 103
Pop art, 101, **105**
Portraiture, **7-10**, 12, 24, 26, 43
Post-impressionism, 44, 72
Powers, Hiram, 29
Precisionists, 74
Prendergast, Maurice, 46, **72**, 73
Primary structure, 105
Primitivism, **7-11**, 103
Prud'hon, Pierre Paul, 11
Psychoanalysis, 100-101

Quidor, John, 28

Realism, The New American, 101, **105**
Realists, New York, 28, **72-73**, 74, **76, 77**
Regionalism, 28, **76-77**, 101, 105
Religious subjects, 7, 10, **11-12**, 24
Rembrandt van Ryn, 26, 72
Renoir, Pierre Auguste, 46
Representational art, 73, **100**, 101, 102, 105
Rimmer, William, 29
Rivera, Diego, 77
Robinson, Theodore, 45
Robus, Hugo, 75

Rodin, Auguste, 47
Romanticism, 11, 12, 24-26, 42, **43-44,** 101
Romney, George, 10, 45
Roszak, Theodore, 104
Rothko, Mark, 103
Rush, William, 8, **11**
Russell, Morgan, 73
Ryder, Albert P., **43-44**, 46, 47, 75

Saint-Gaudens, Augustus, 47
Sargent, Henry, 26
Sargent, John S., 44, **45**
Schamberg, Morton L., 74
Schmidt, Katherine, 77
Sculpture, **10-11**, 29, 47, 75, **103-104**
Seligmann, Kurt, 101
Shahn, Ben, 77, **100**
Sheeler, Charles, 74
Shinn, Everett, 72
Shirlaw, Walter, 45
Siqueiros, David Alfaro, 77
Sloan, John, **72**, 76, **100**
Smibert, John, **7**, 8
Social school, 75, **77, 100,** 101, 102
Soyer, Raphael, 77
Stella, Joseph, 72, **74**
Sterne, Maurice, 72
Stieglitz, Alfred, 72
Stijl, De, 102
Still-life, 28-29
Storrs, John, 75
Stuart, Gilbert, 10
Sully, Thomas, 10, 12
Surrealism, **101,** 102-103
Synchromism, 73

Tanguy, Yves, 101
Thayer, Abbott H., **46,** 47
Thorwaldsen, Albert Bertel, 29
Tobey, Mark, 103
Traditionalists, **11-12**, 28, 29, 44, **46-47,** 72, 75, 100
Trompe l'oeil, 28-29
Trumbull, John, **11-12**, 24
Twachtman, John, 45-46

Vanderlyn, John, 12, 24
Vedder, Elihu, 47
Velázquez, Diego de Silva y, 44, 45, 72

Walkowitz, Abraham, 74
Weber, Max, **73**, 74, **75**, 76
Weir, J. Alden, 45
West, Benjamin, 9, **11**, 43
Whistler, James A. McNeill, **44-45**, 47
Wimar, Charles, 26
Winstanley, William, 24
Wood, Grant, 76
Wood, Thomas Waterman, 28
Woodville, Richard Caton, 26
Wyant, Alexander H., 42

Zorach, William, 73, **75**